I0393800

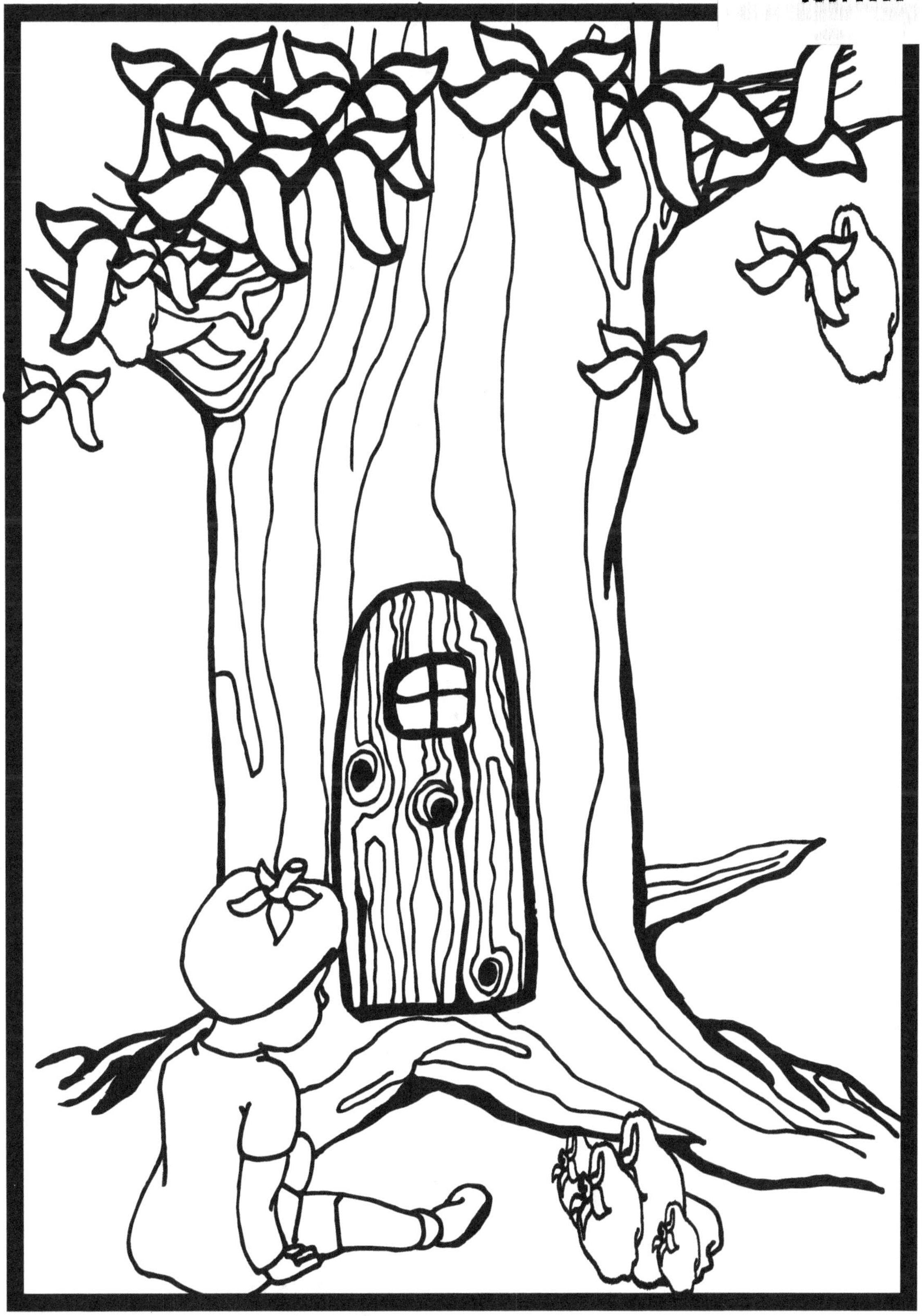

Johnny Appleseed planted 100,000 apple trees

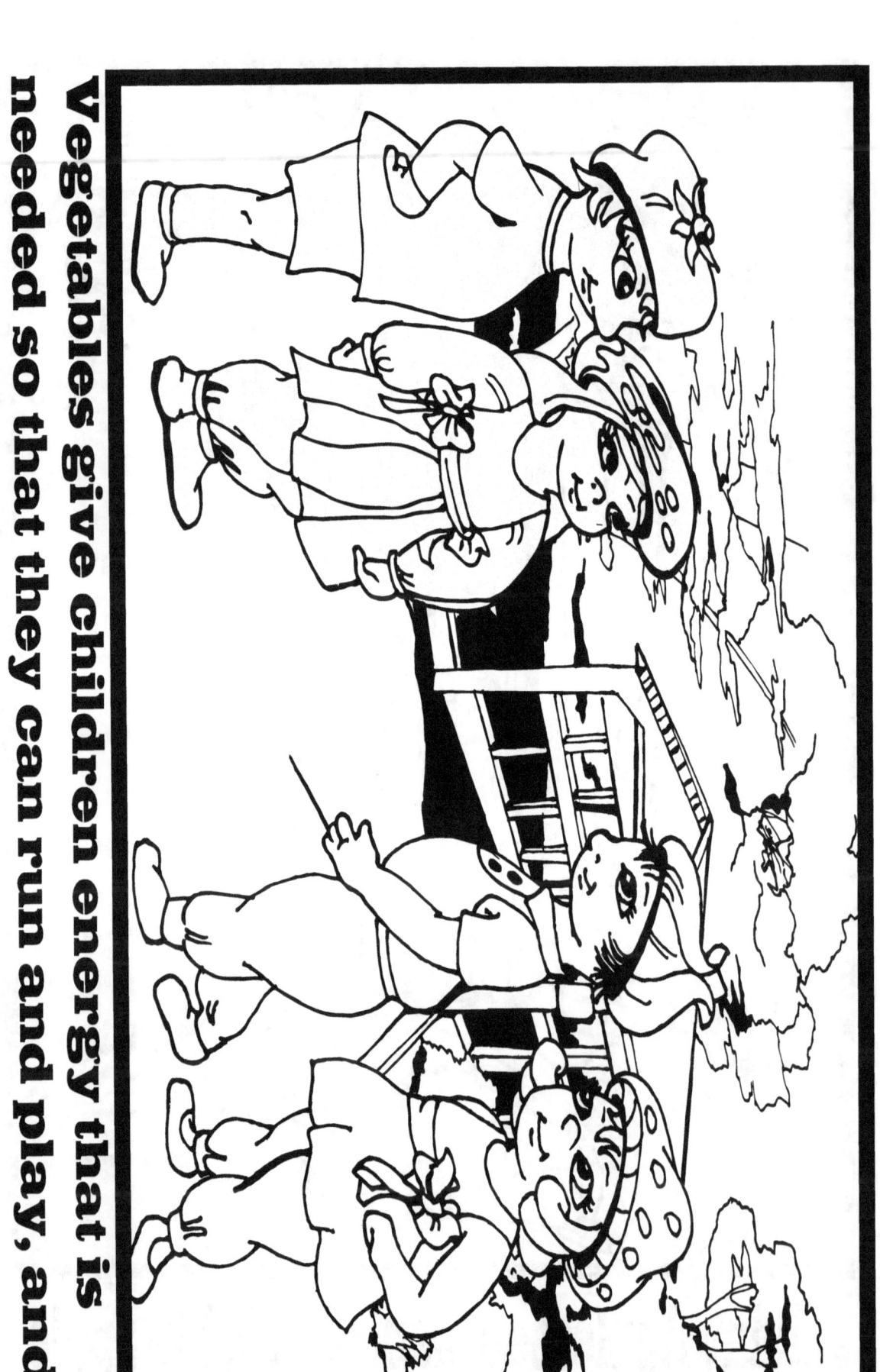

Vegetables give children energy that is needed so that they can run and play, and discover new worlds.

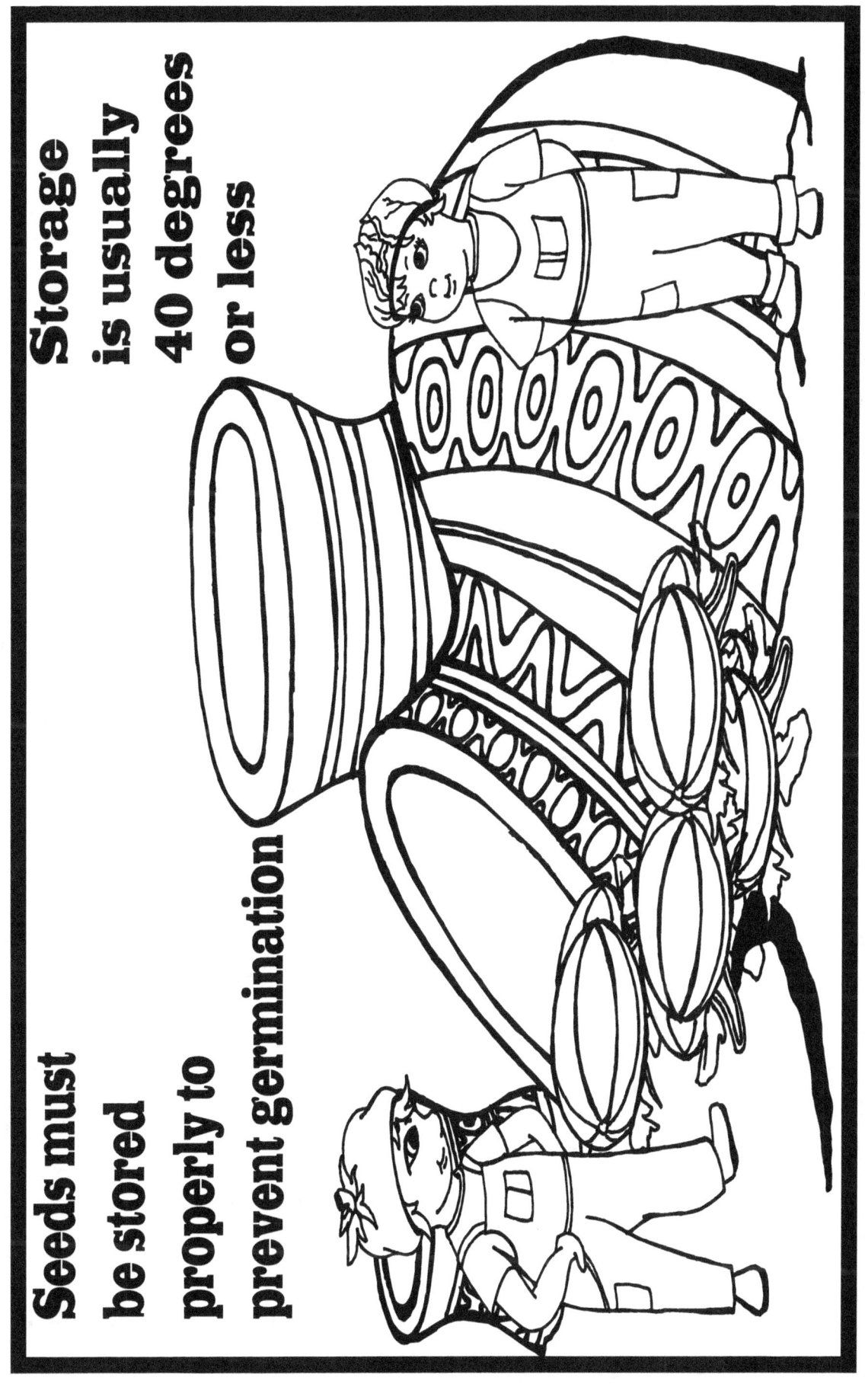

Seeds must
be stored
properly to
prevent germination

Storage
is usually
40 degrees
or less

In 2005, the largest apple ever produced weighed 4-pounds 1-ounce.

There are 7-thousand varieties world-wide.

The water content of an apple is 84%.

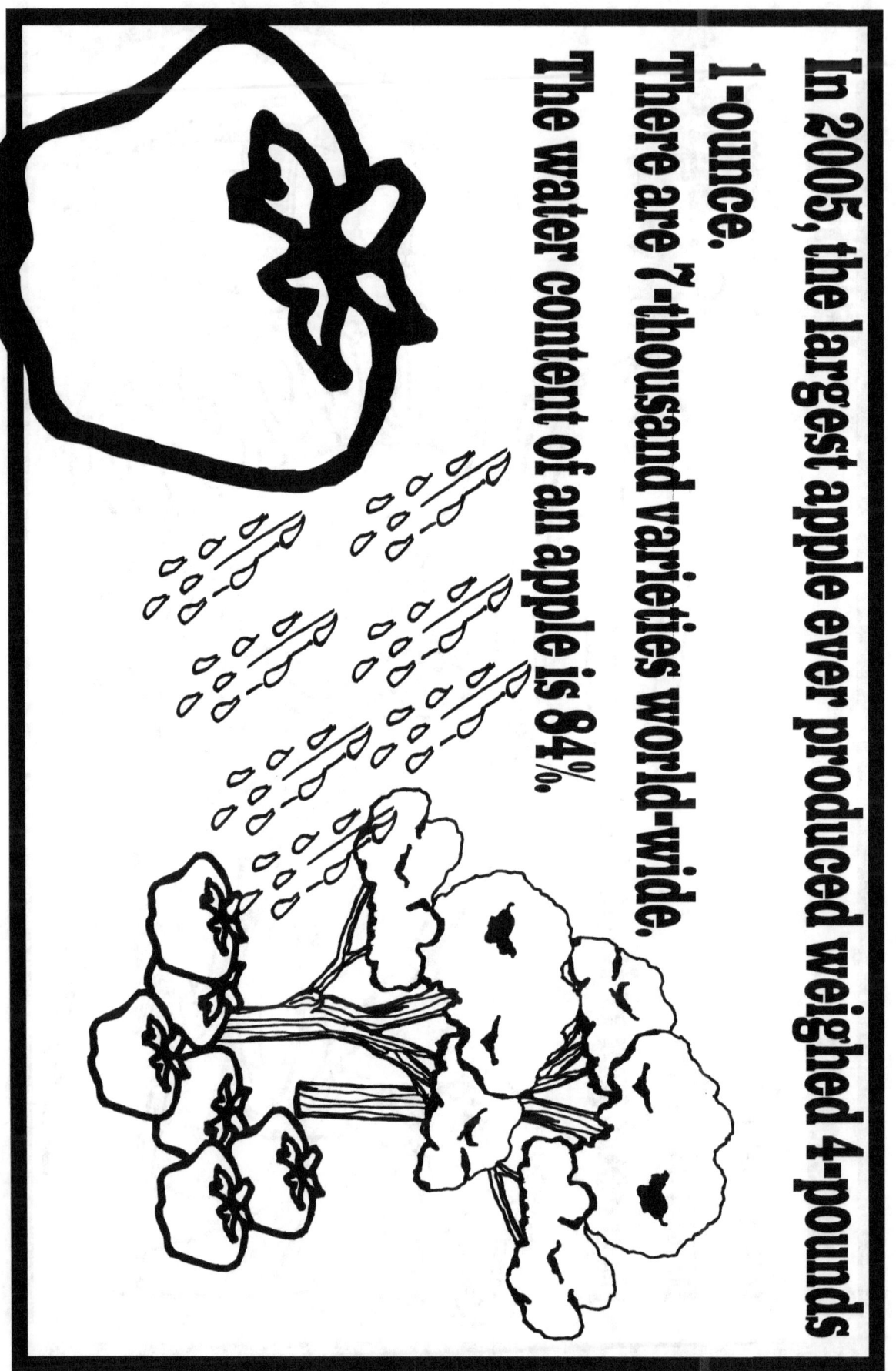

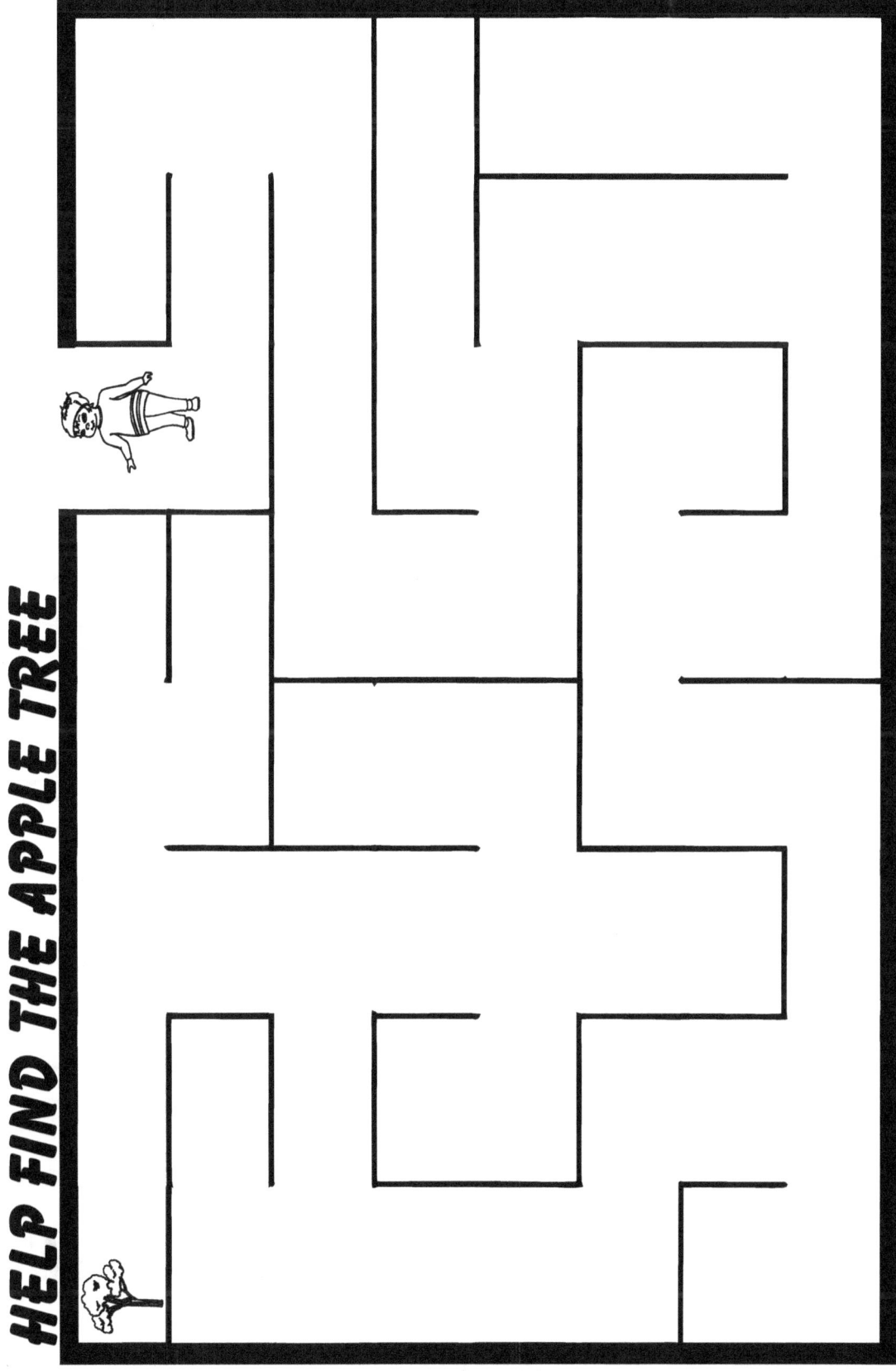

HELP FIND THE APPLE TREE

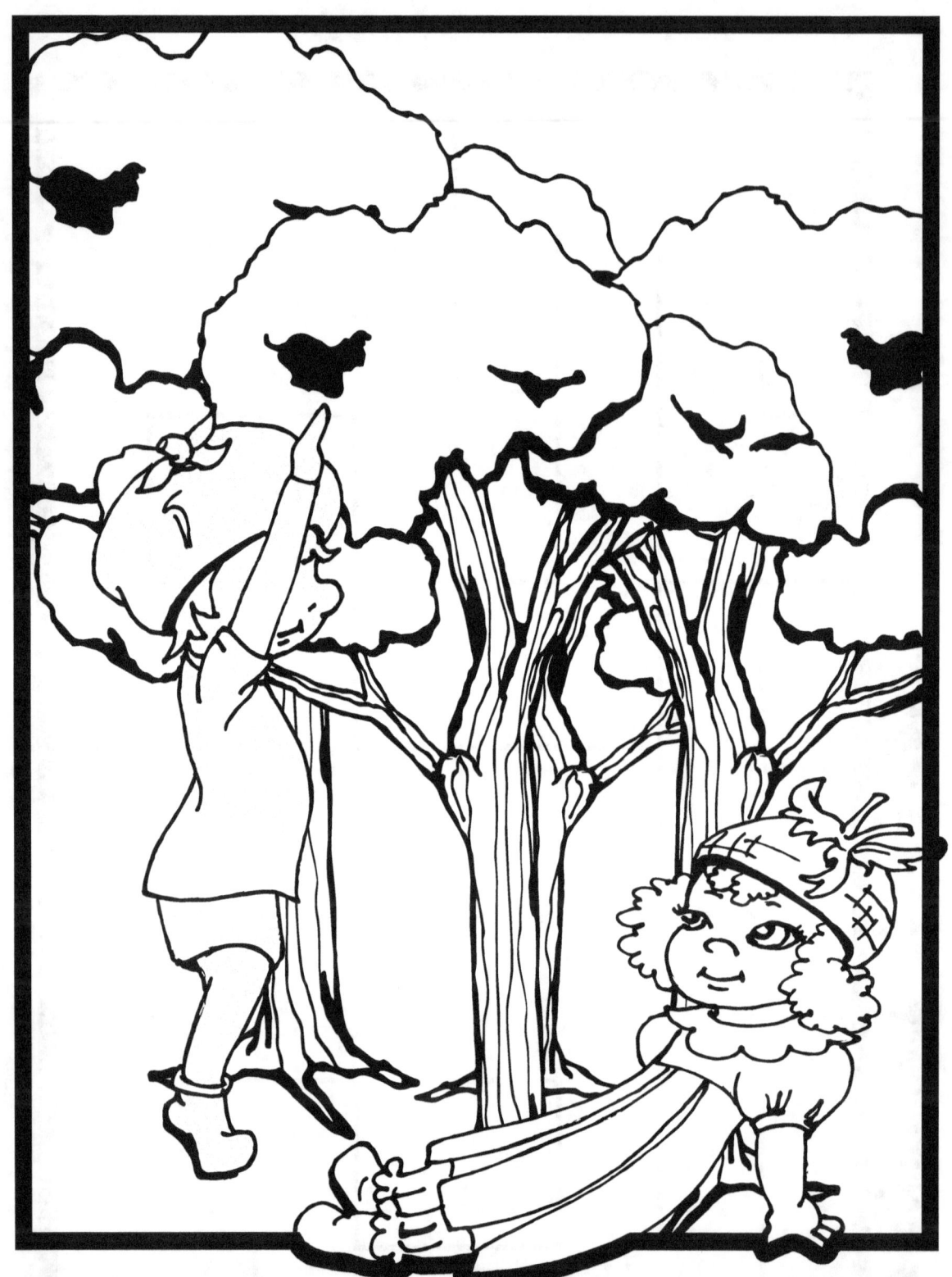

Because apples are loaded with air, approximately 25%, they will float in water.

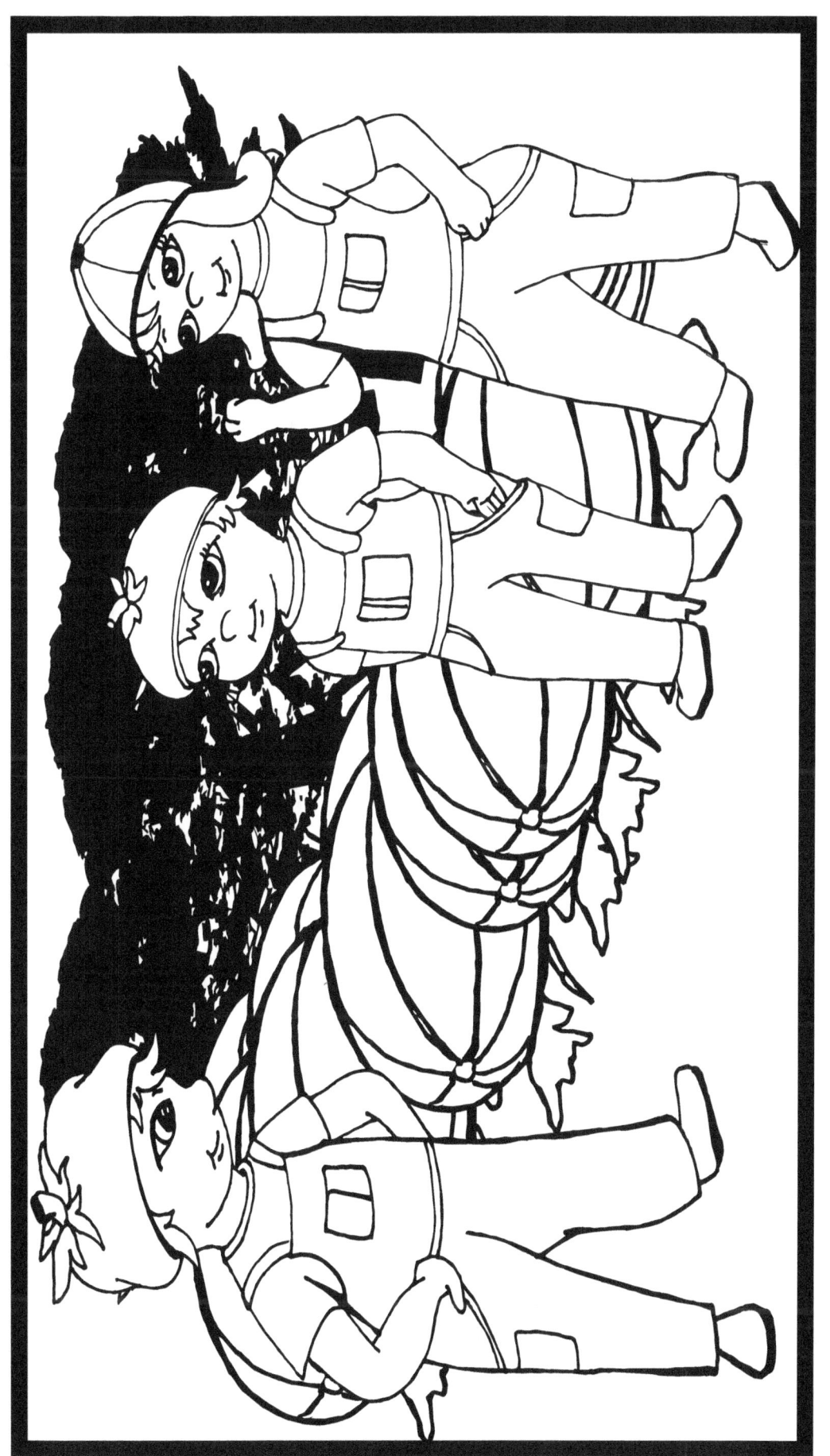

Watermelons grow best in sandy soil.

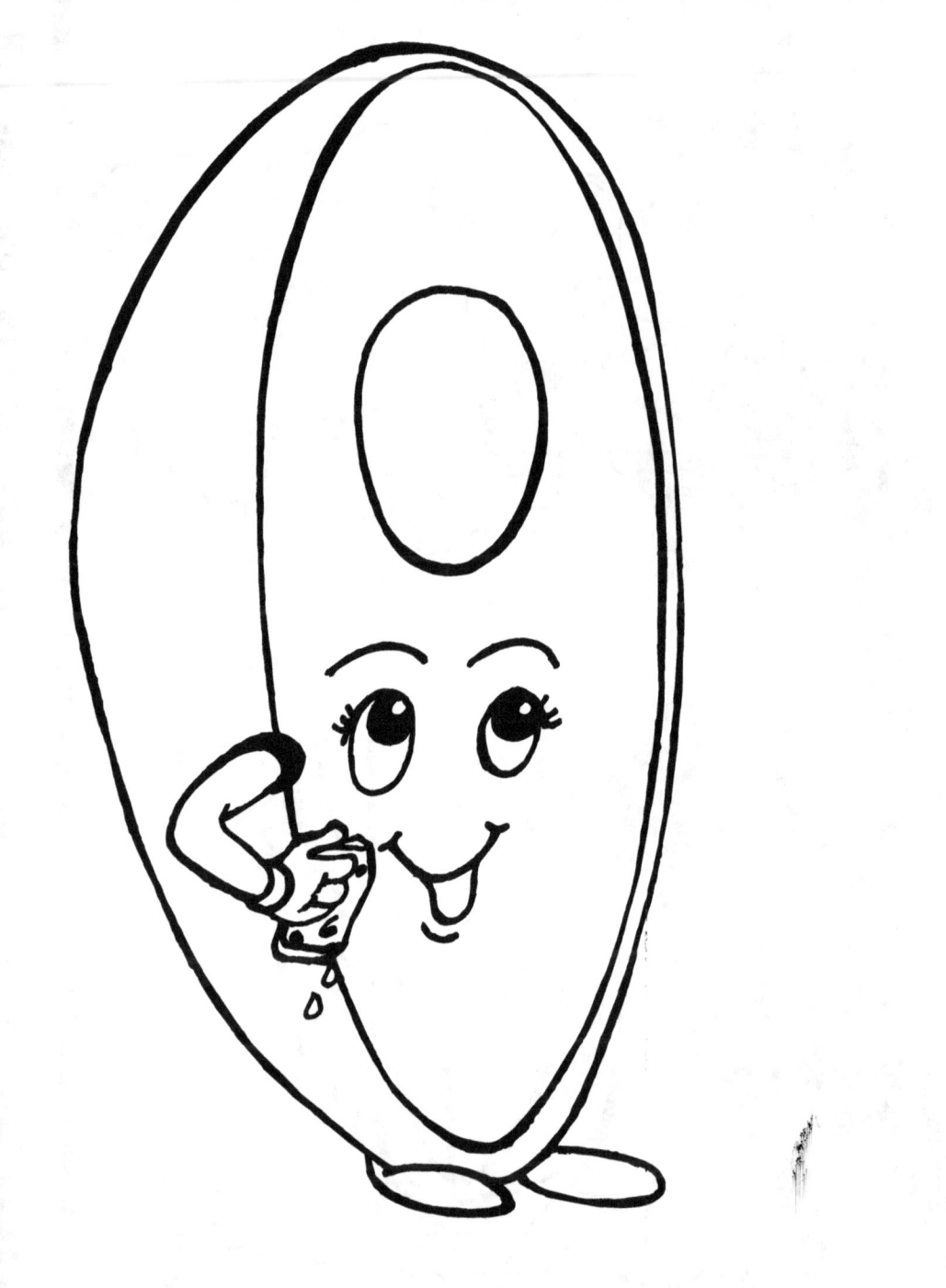

Avocado acts a s a sponge in the body to absorb more nutrients.

Find and circle Baby spud

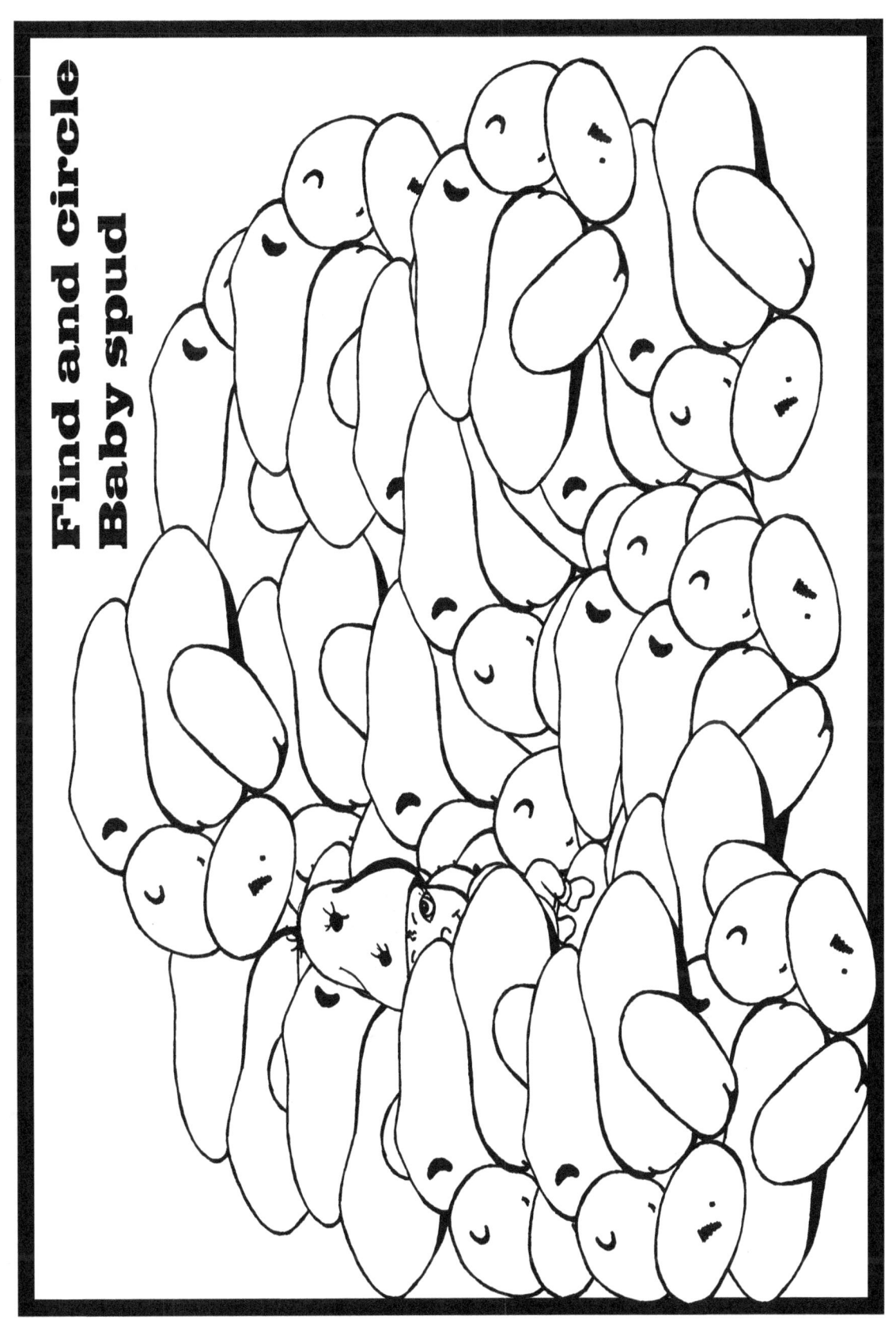

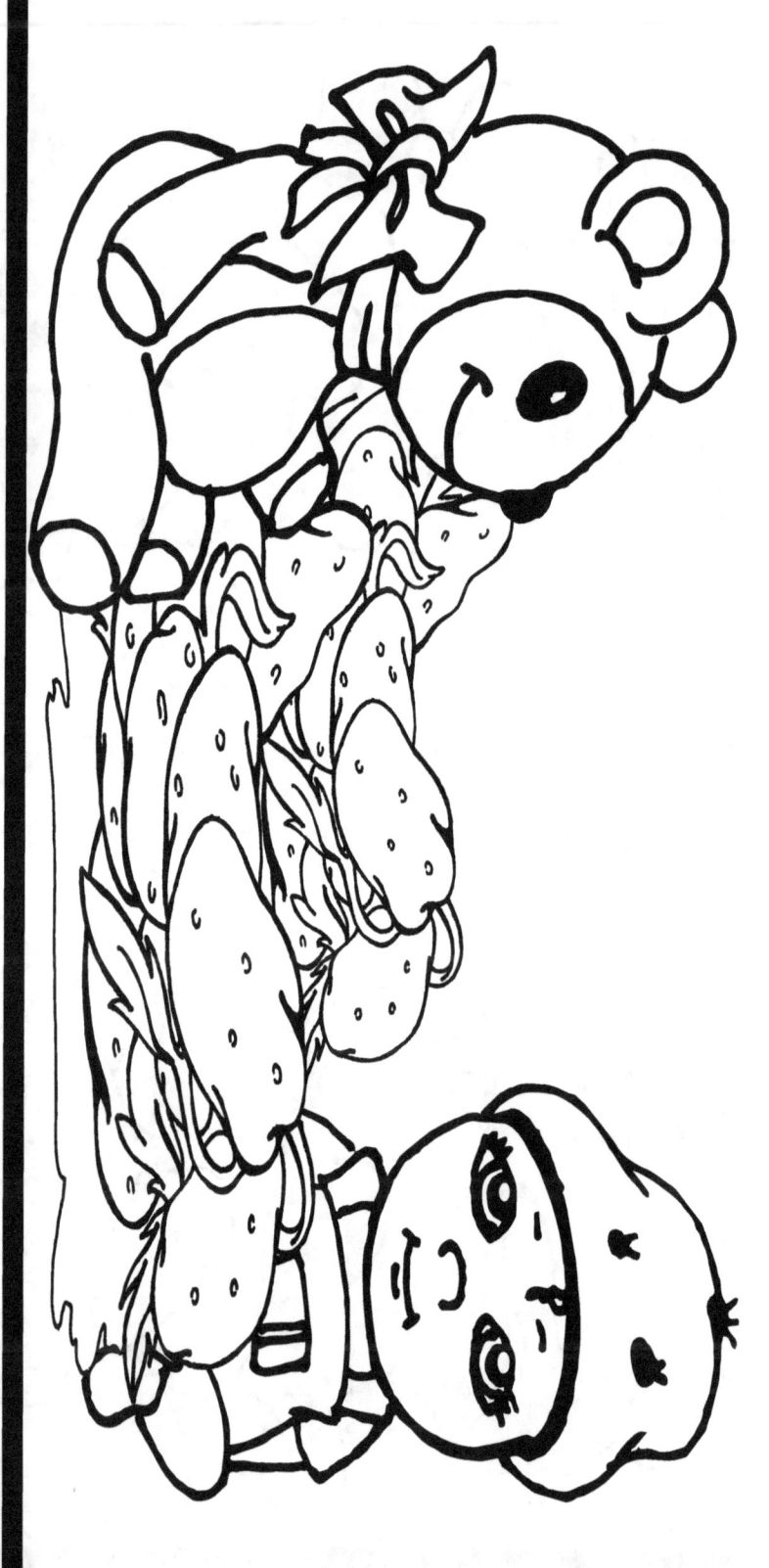

Although the potato comes from the Andean Mountian region of South America, it was first brough to North America by Irish immigrants.

The average person eats 73-lbs of potatoes yearly.

The hole that is dug in preparation for planting potatoes is called a "Spud." However, the term has come to mean an immature or underdeveloped potato.

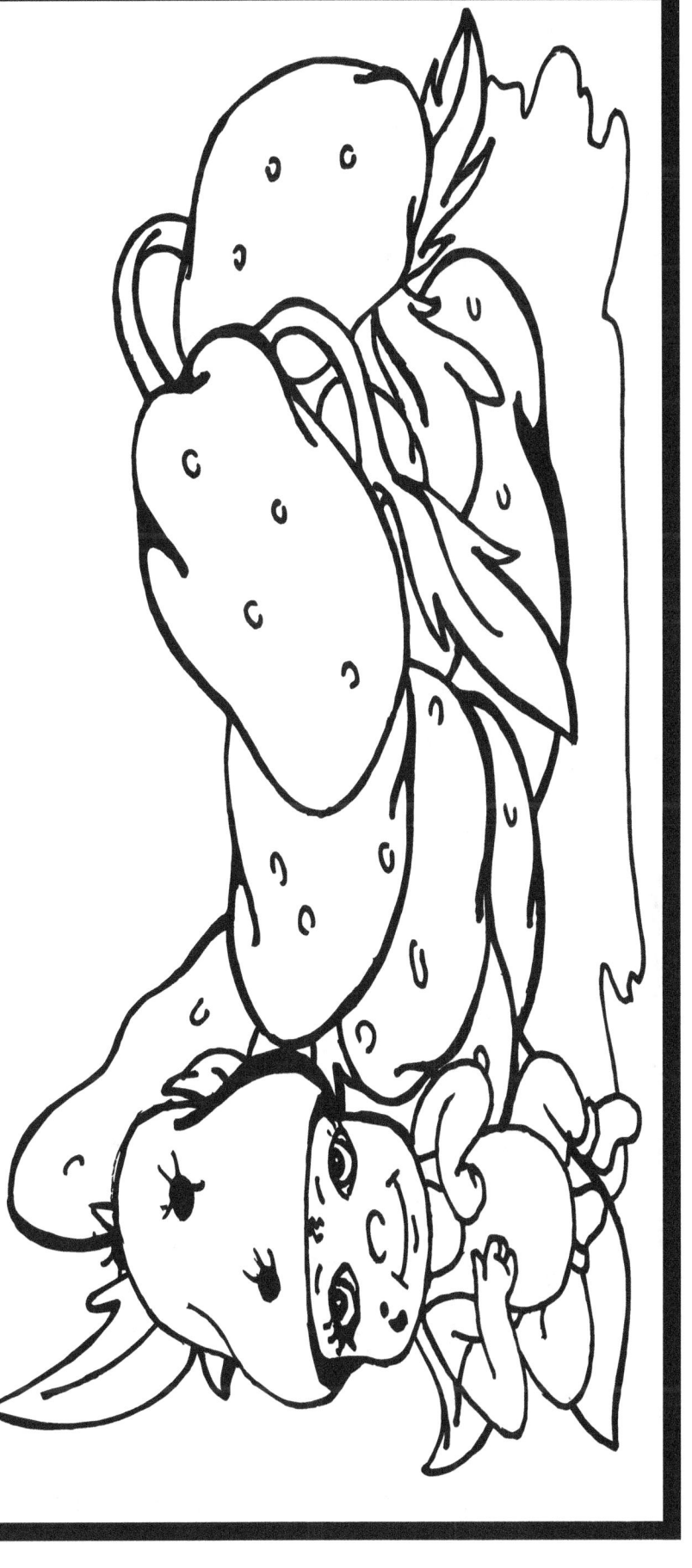

Potatoes are a healthy vegetable as long as they are not fired and smothered in fatty dairy products. Mashed and roasted potatoes are much healthier and supply a greater nutritional balance.

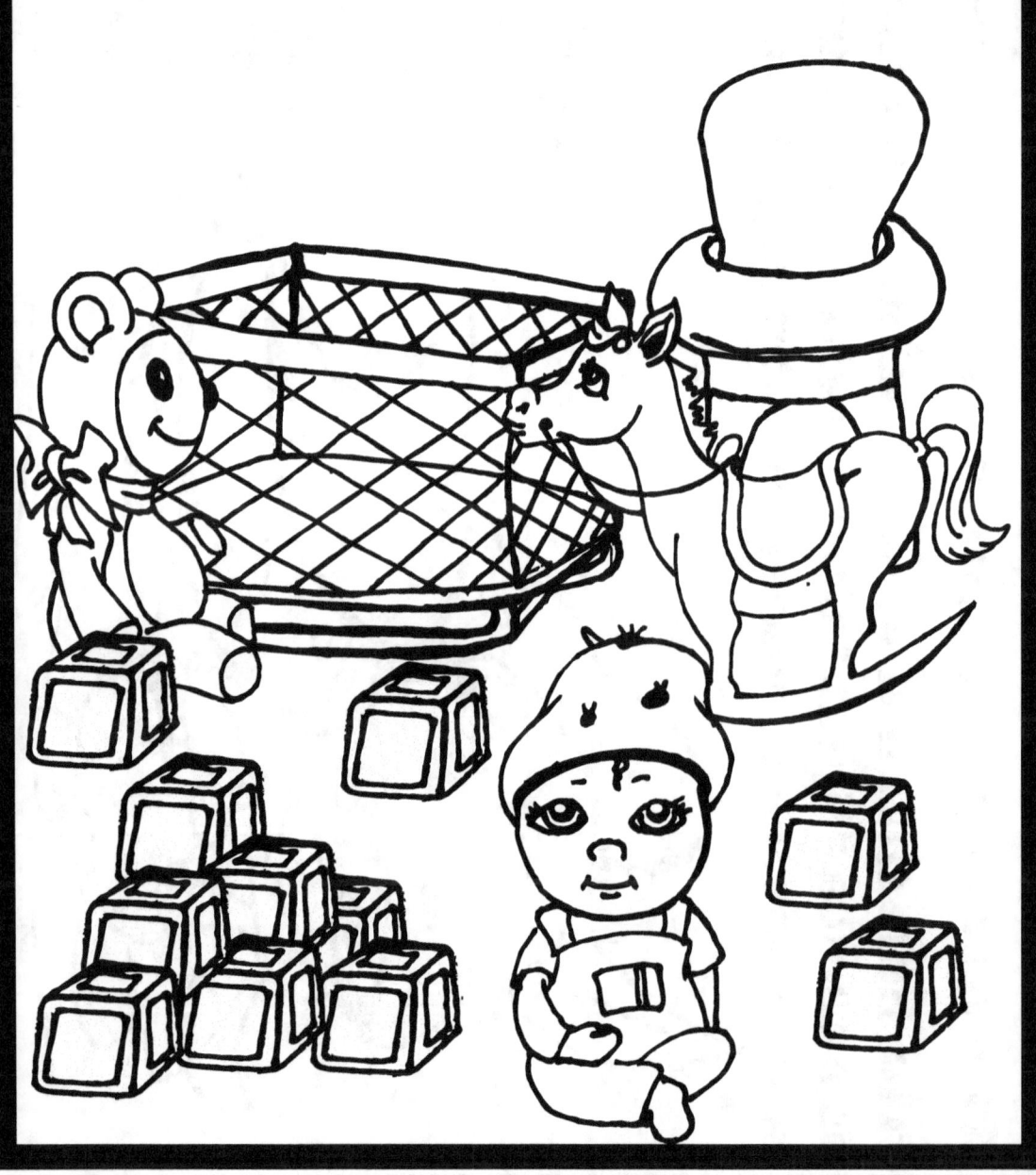

Although broccoli is a vegetable, it is also a flower.

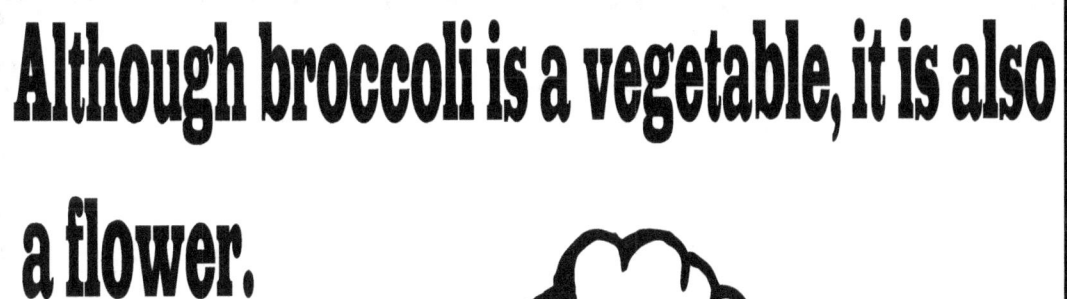

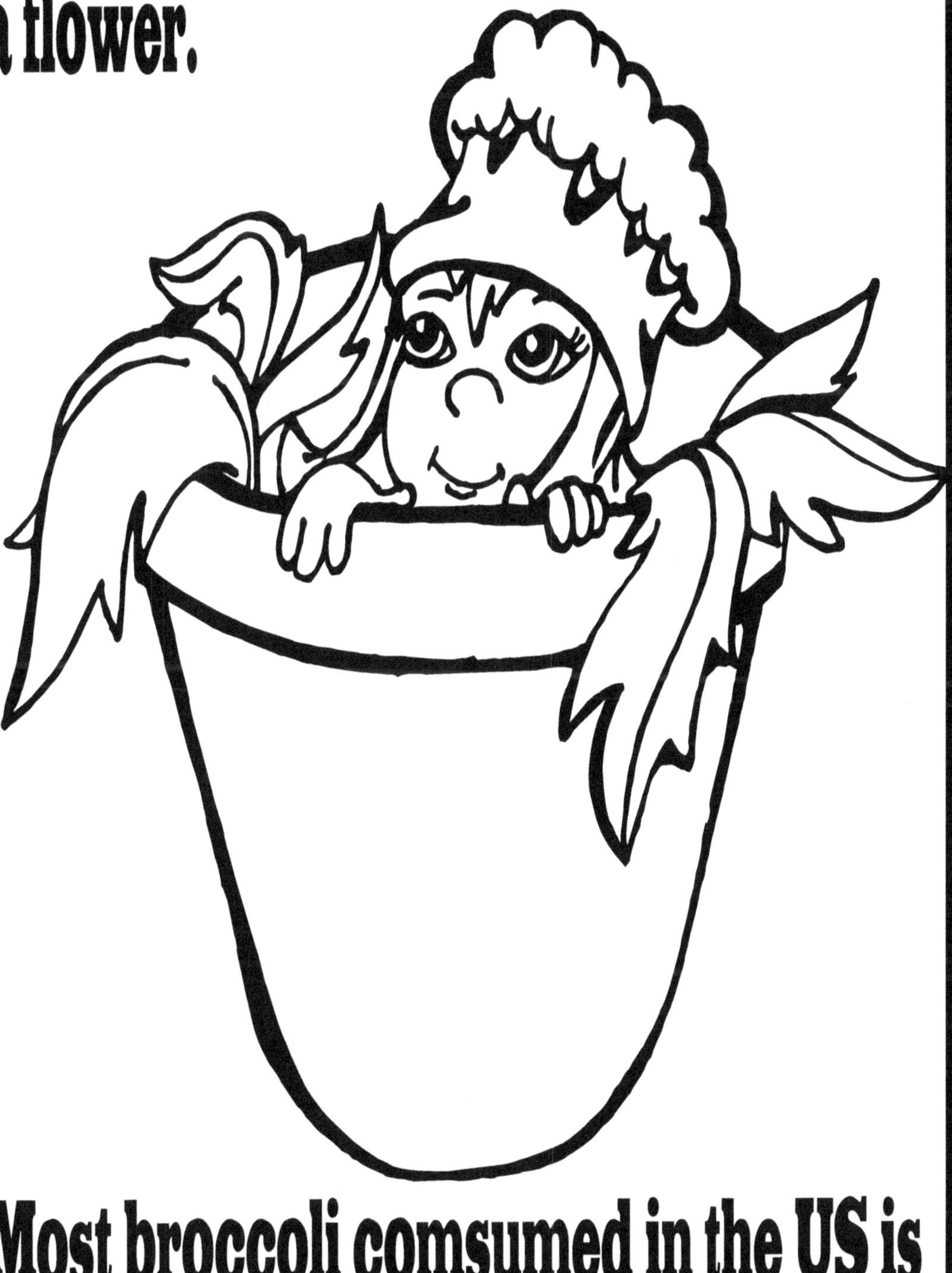

Most broccoli comsumed in the US is produced in California.

Beets help to rebuild tissue and strengthen bones and teeth.

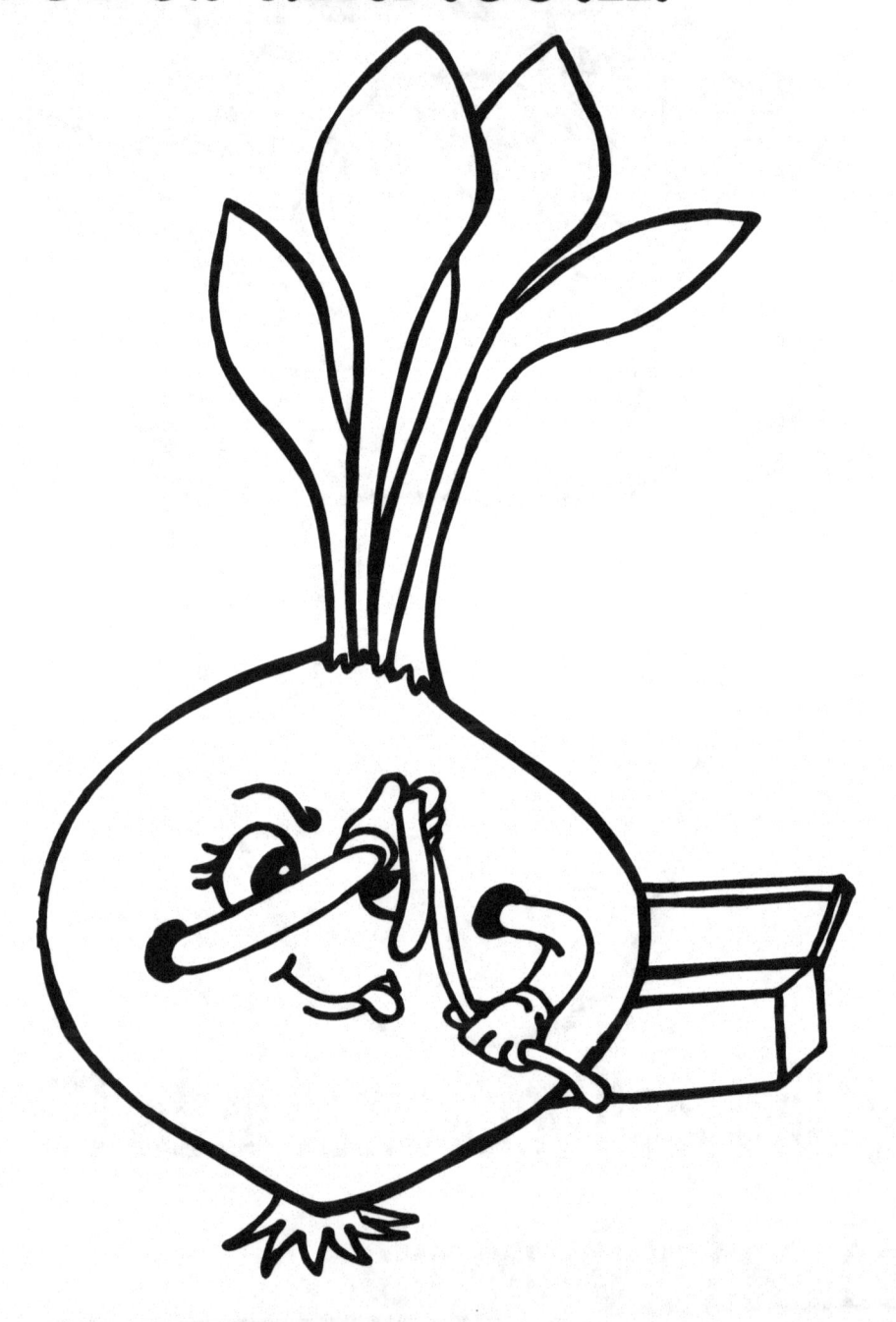

The Chinese eat a lot of broccoli,

as much as

8-million

tons

per year!

The largest

broccoli

ever produced

was 28 pounds

Broccoli

was

called

Calabrese

in the

Calabria

Provence

where it

was first

grown

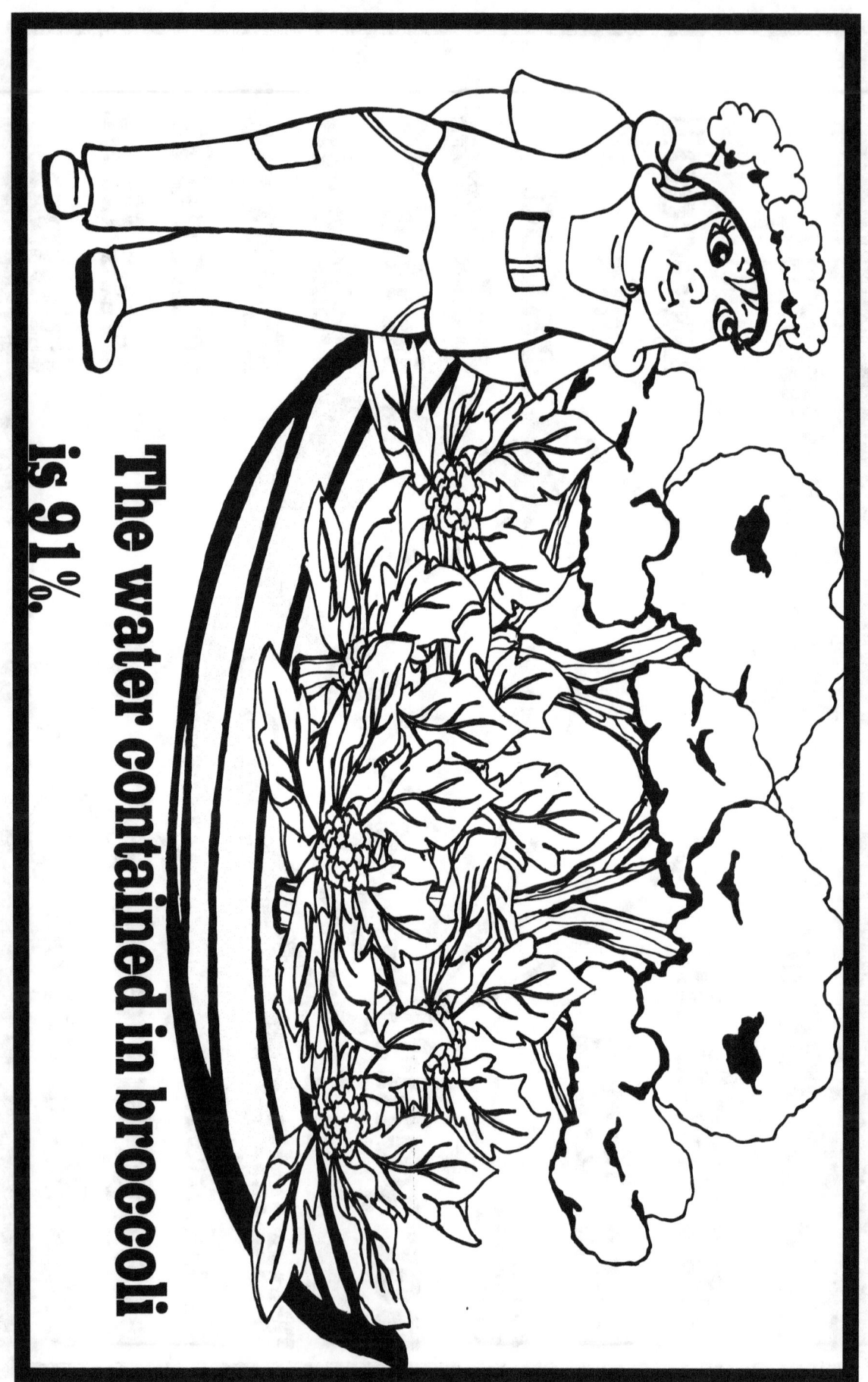

The water contained in broccoli is 91%.

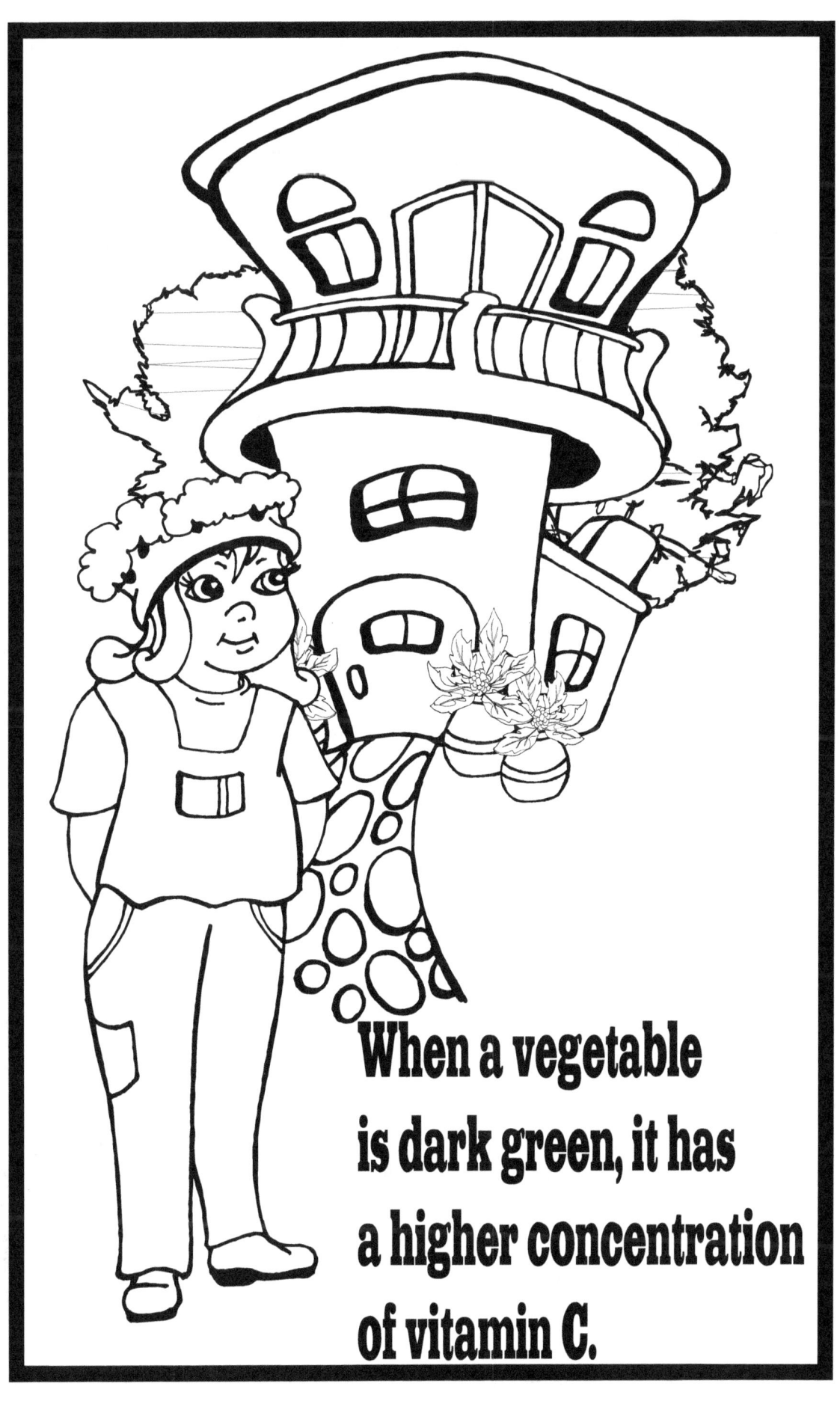

When a vegetable
is dark green, it has
a higher concentration
of vitamin C.

It might surprise you to learn that the Butter bean can reduce your risk of heart attack by 82%...that's a big win-win

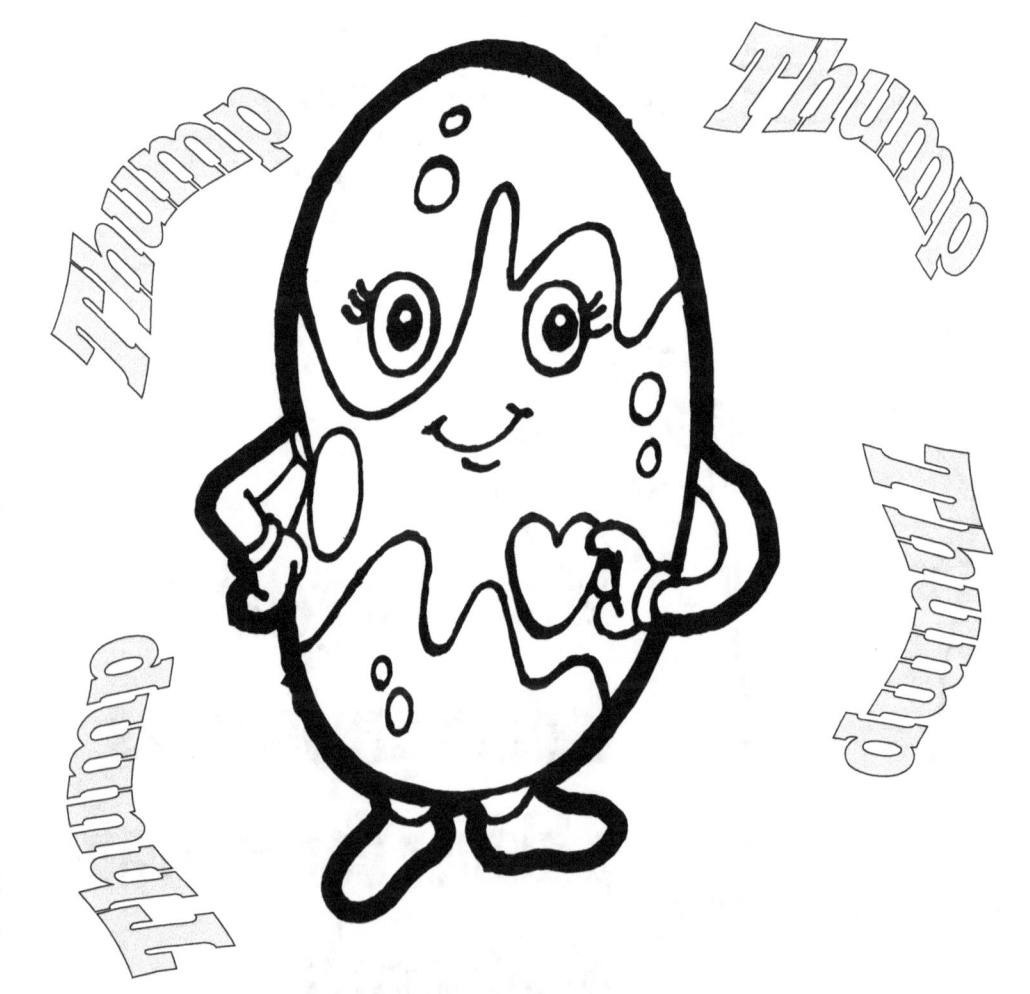

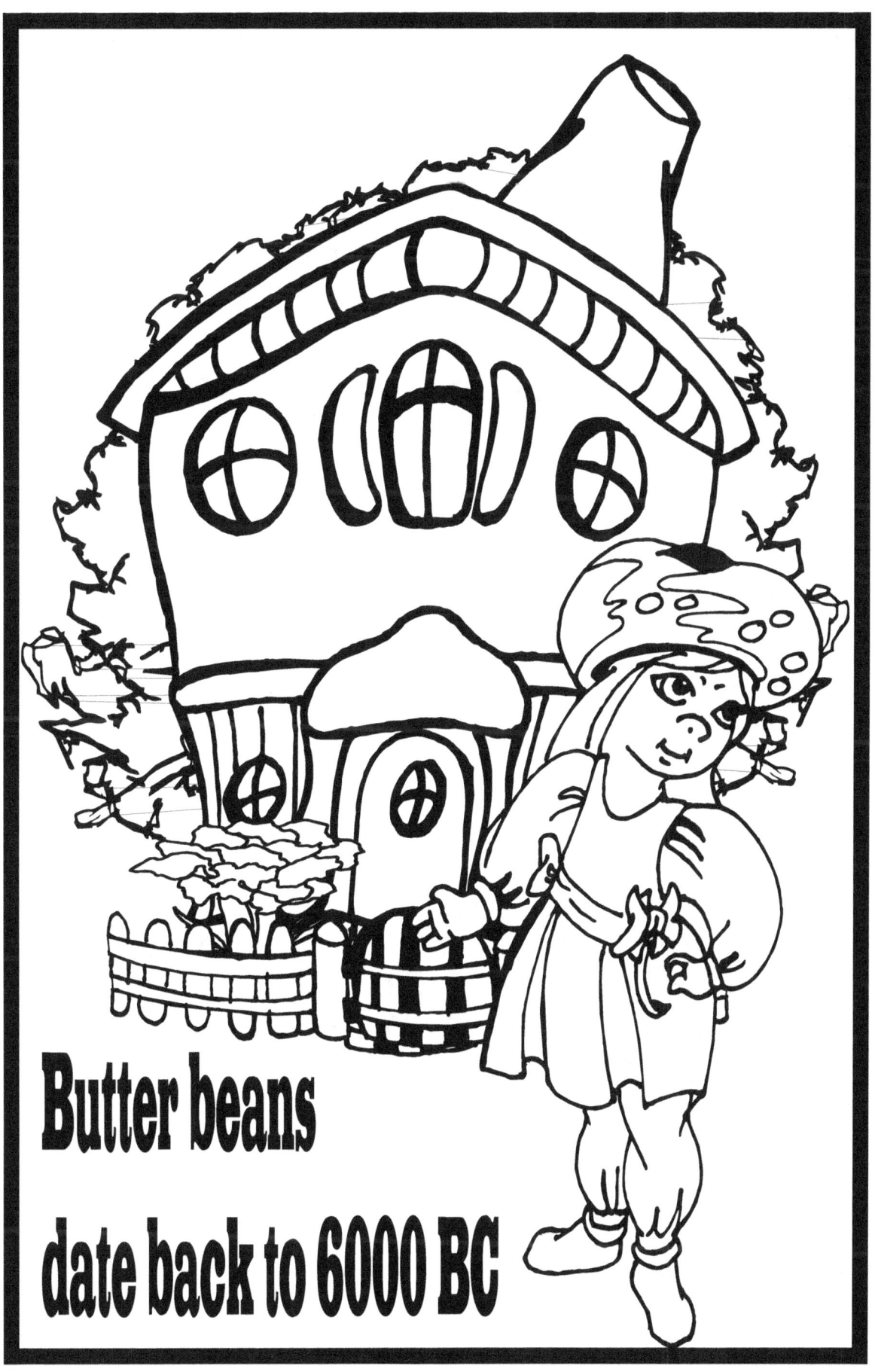

Butter beans date back to 6000 BC

Linamarin a property of butter beans makes the beans unsafe to eat raw.

There are three varities of Butter Beans (also known as lima beans):

Large, or Specked Butter beans

Medium, or Ford Hooks

Small, or Baby Lima.

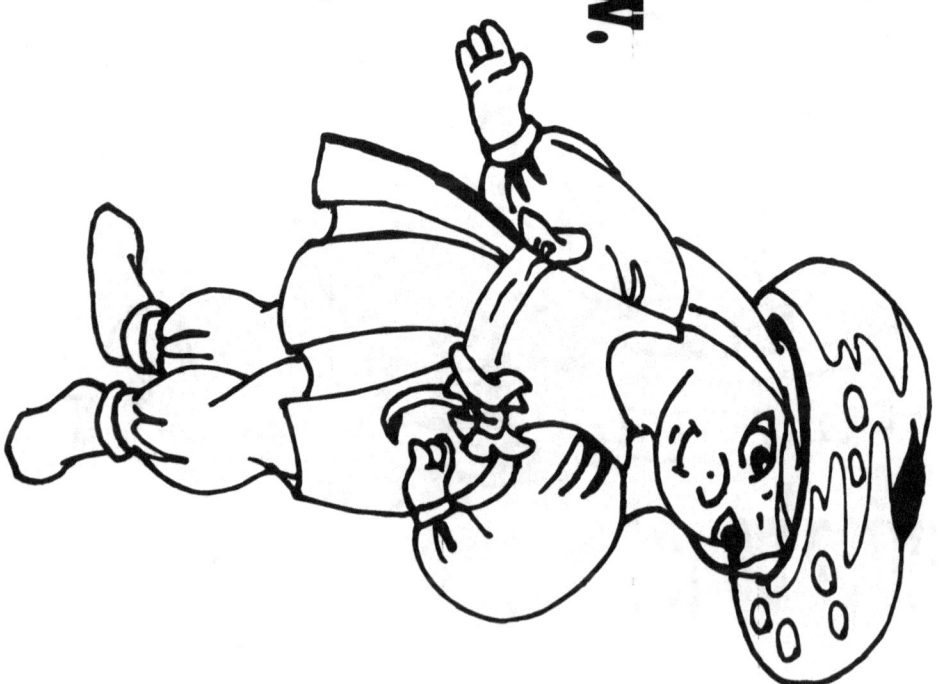

Almost as important
as corn, butter beans
were a major staple of the
Native American
culture.

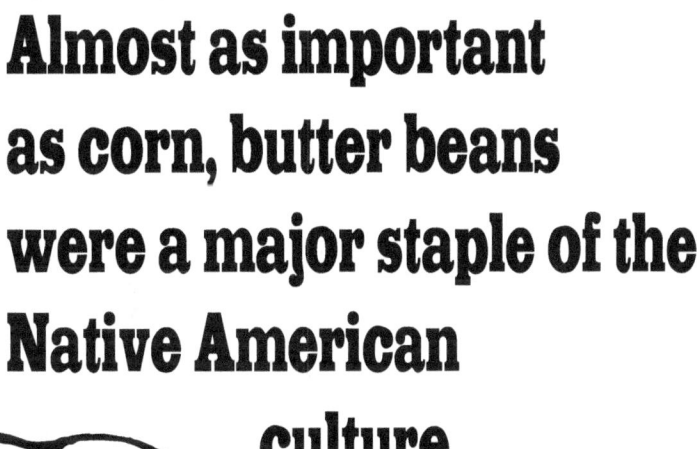

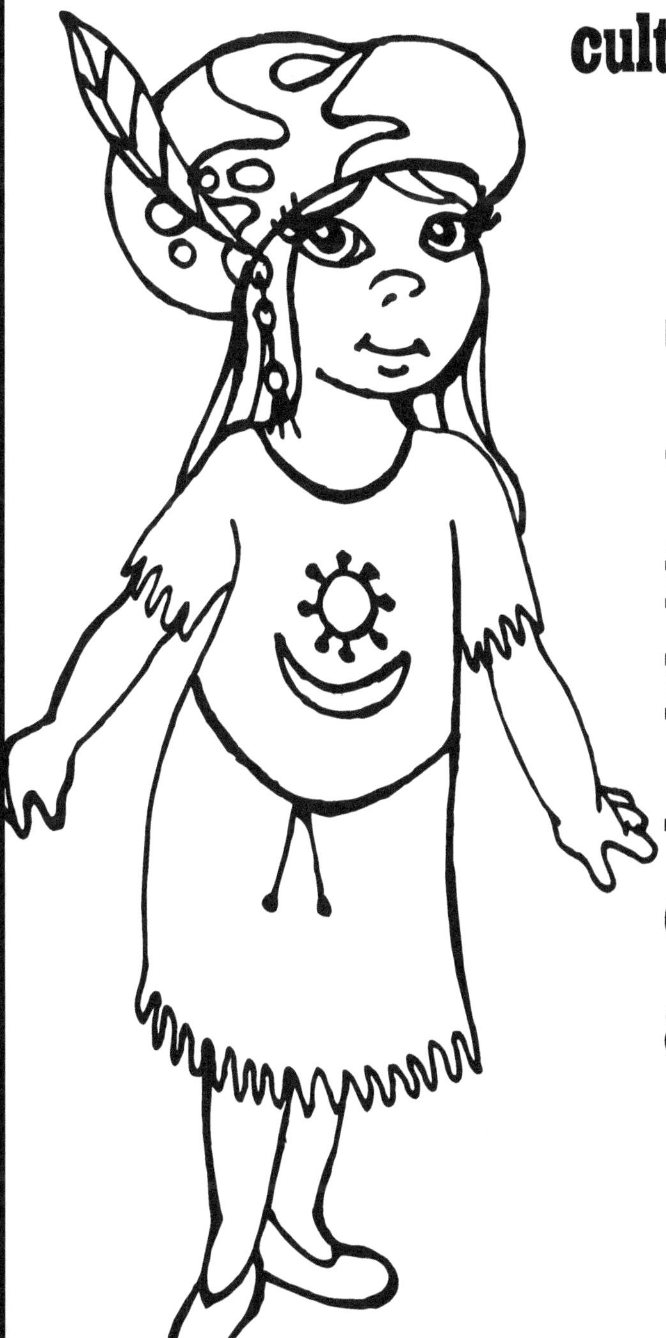

They
were
found in
North
American
culture
as early as
1301

To stay healthy, children need sunshine fresh air, and exercise.

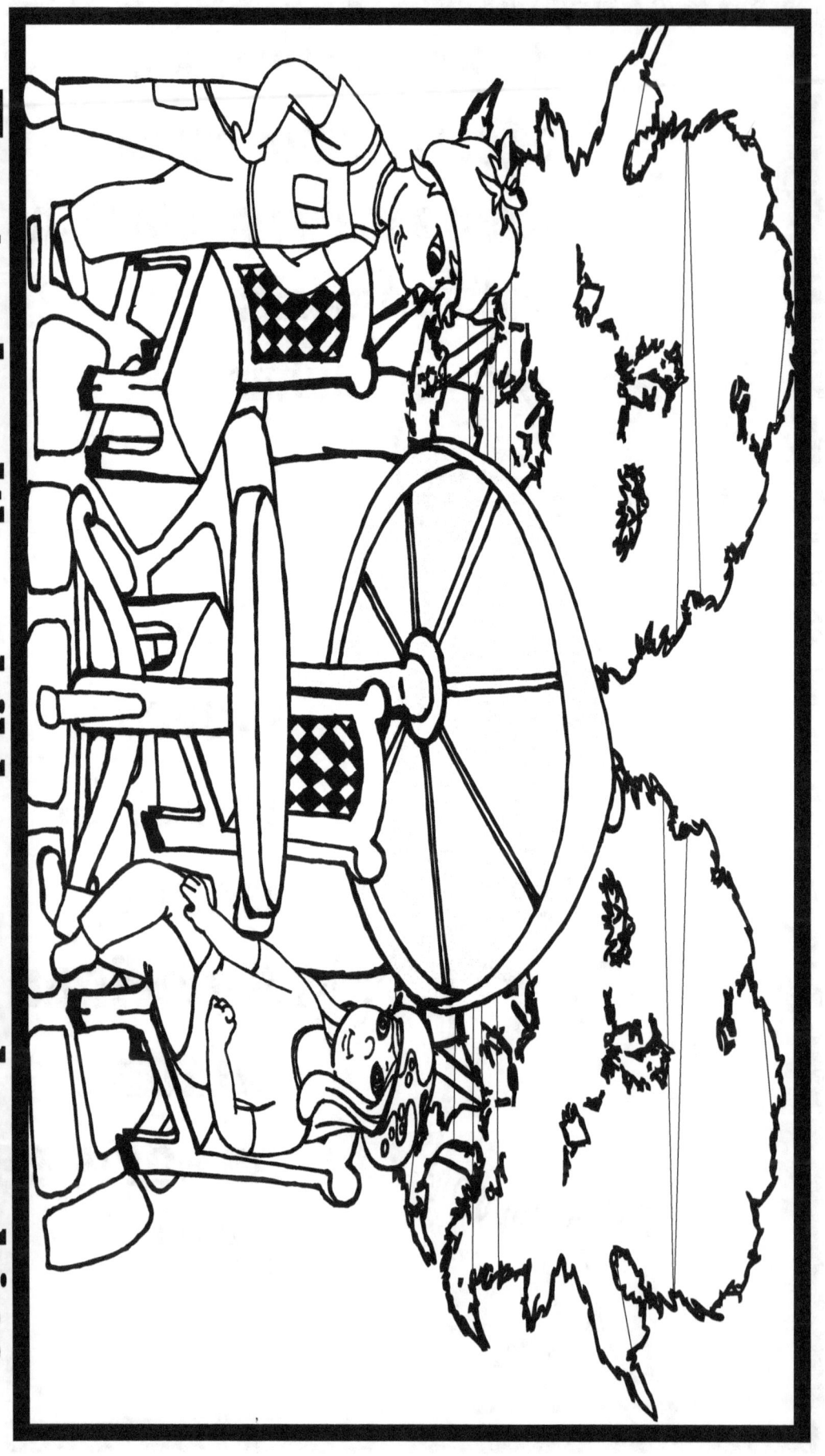

B	U	T	T	E	R	B	E	A	N
O	R	M	O	S	T	Q	M	B	T
K	V	O	A	G	E	D	A	C	E
H	B	O	C	G	H	A	U	T	T
R	O	R	A	C	A	R	R	O	T
X	J	H	B	R	O	B	J	R	B
L	O	S	B	C	E	L	E	R	Y
L	Q	U	A	B	V	C	I	G	Q
E	V	M	G	B	M	P	V	A	W
T	R	F	E	S	N	K	L	R	X
T	V	F	C	G	P	U	T	L	C
U	C	J	H	O	V	U	P	I	H
C	H	A	P	P	L	E	D	C	B
E	Y	K	M	Y	I	R	M	J	G
W	A	T	E	R	M	E	L	O	N
P	W	T	C	G	E	B	Q	P	L

ButterBean's Treat

Cabbage dates back to 4000 B.C. where it was found in China

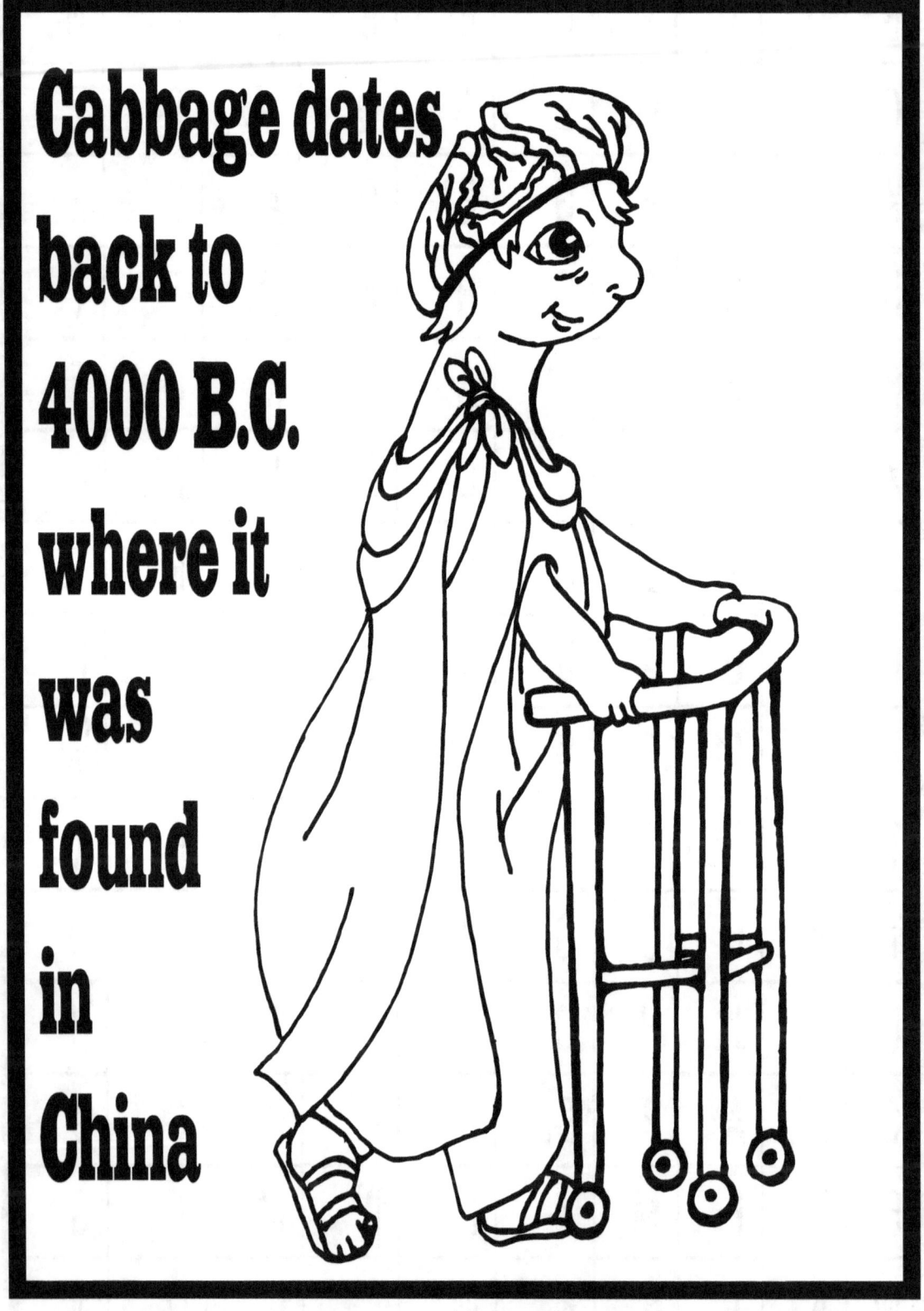

Cabbage is an Old Vegetable

Did you know that the Romans believed cabbage was a very important vegetable, and that in Greek Mythology it is sometimes called "Lycurgus Tears?"

In Scotland cabbage is called "Bowkail." In German it's called "Kohl."

The water content in cabbage is approximately 90%.

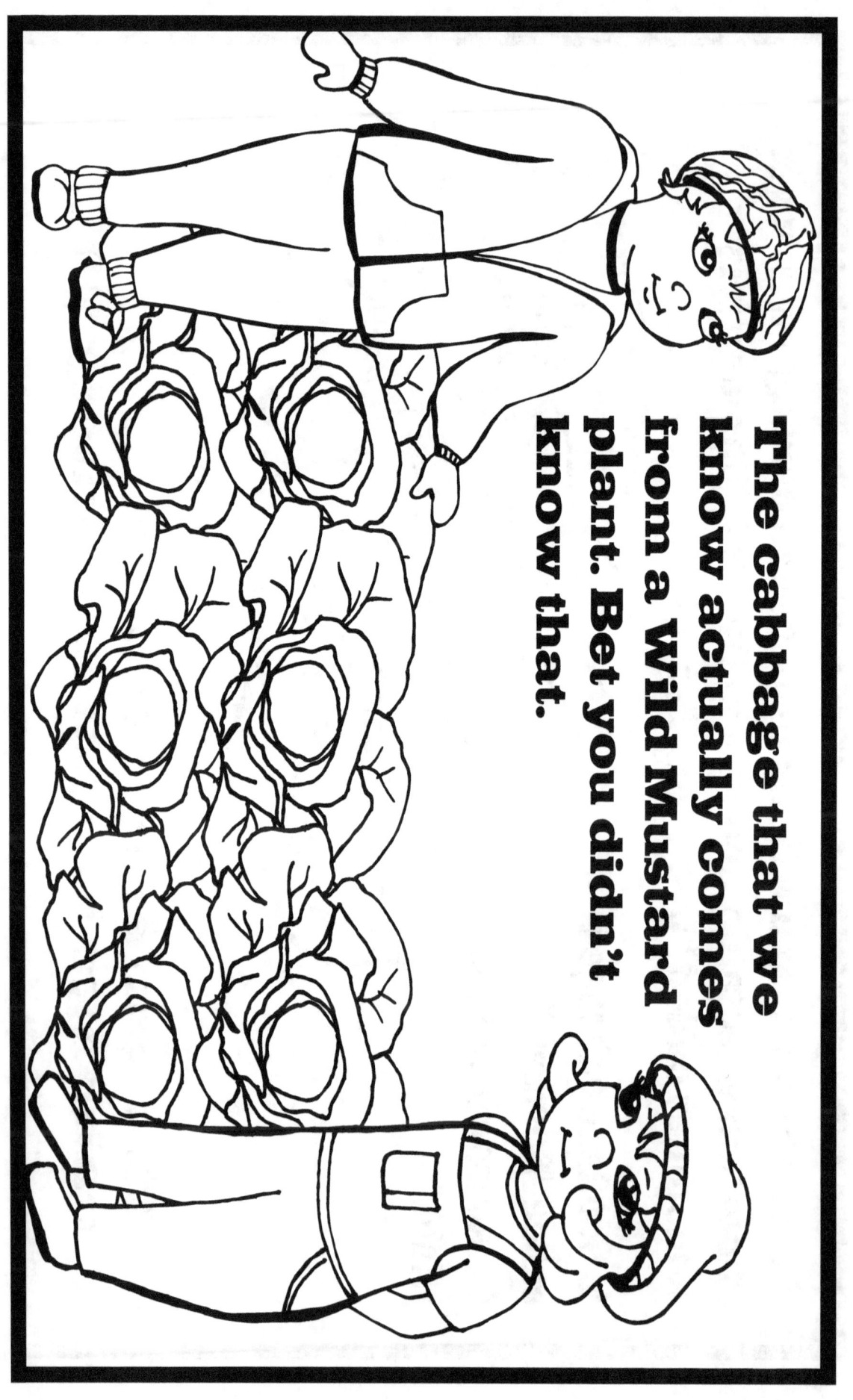

The cabbage that we know actually comes from a Wild Mustard plant. Bet you didn't know that.

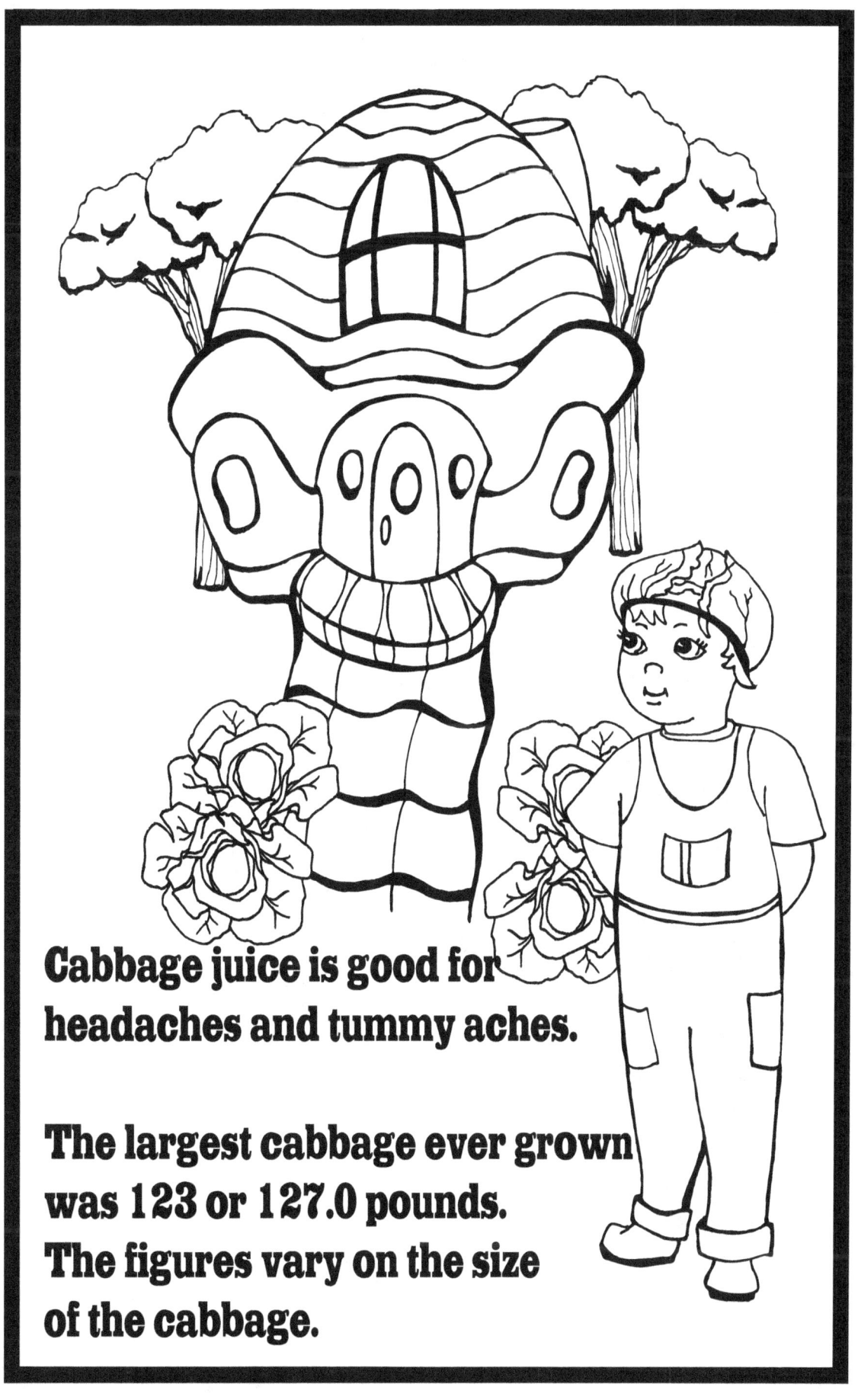

Cabbage juice is good for headaches and tummy aches.

The largest cabbage ever grown was 123 or 127.0 pounds. The figures vary on the size of the cabbage.

Carrots and Celery have properties that help to clean your mouth of bacteria.

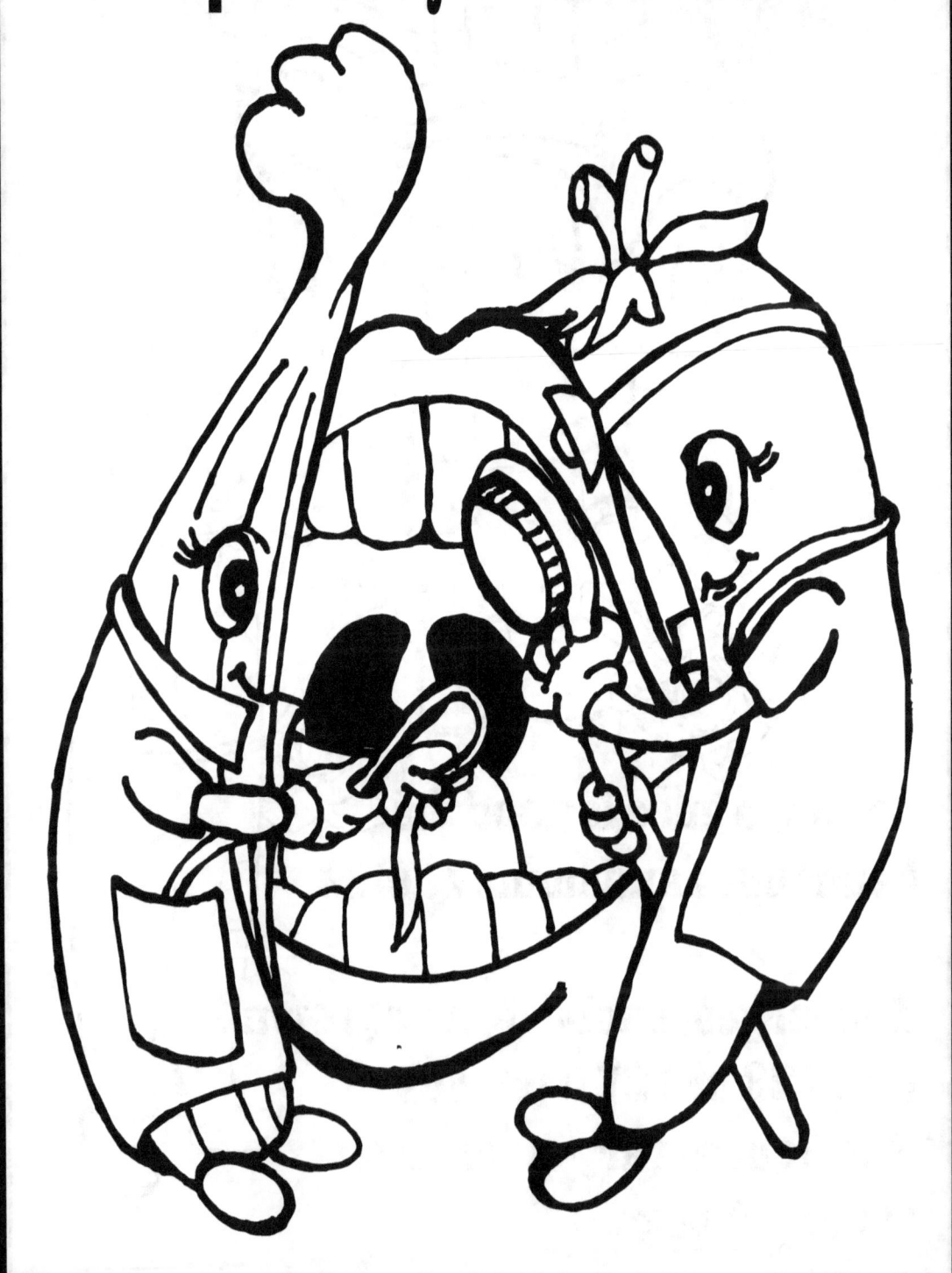

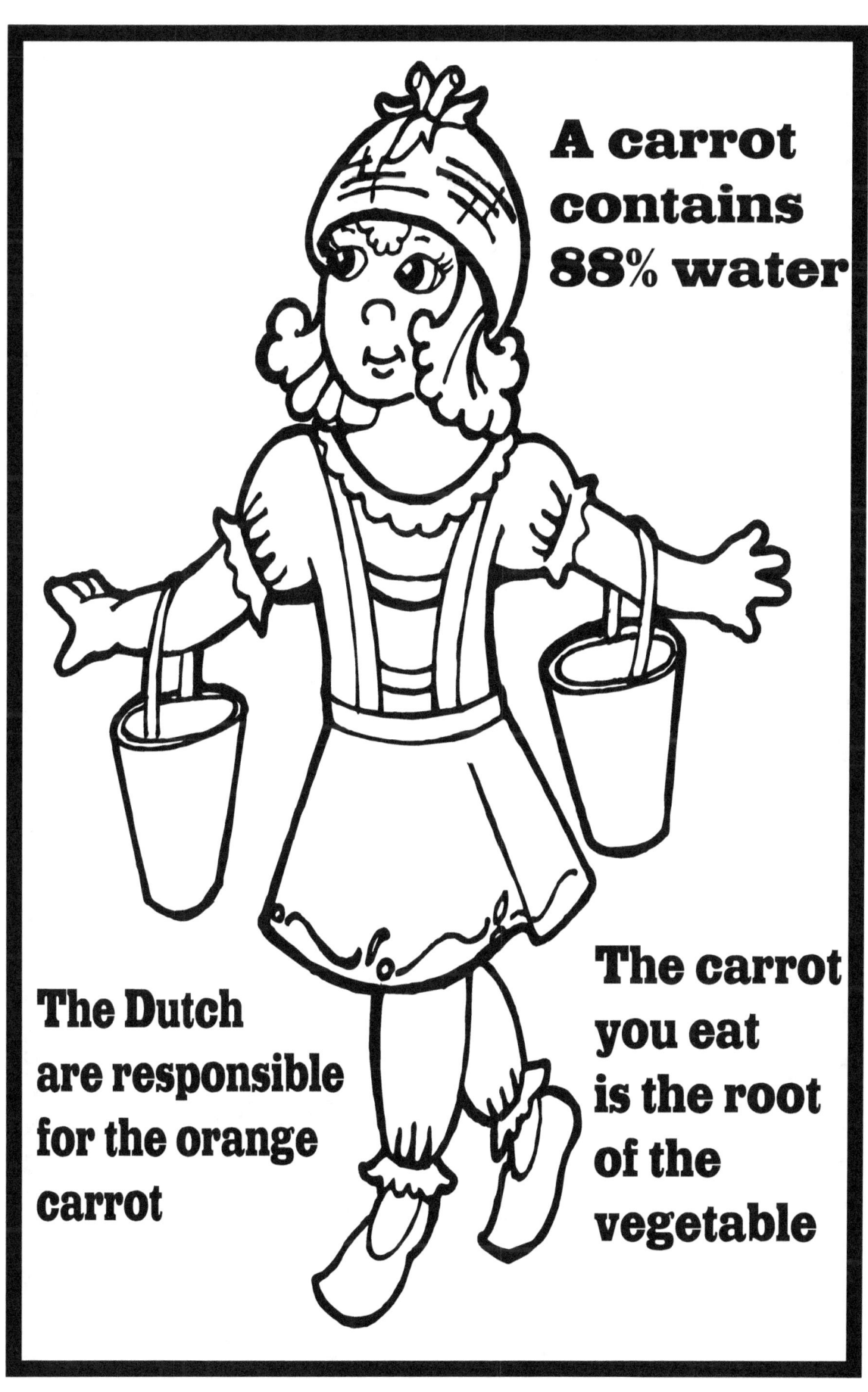

A carrot contains 88% water

The Dutch are responsible for the orange carrot

The carrot you eat is the root of the vegetable

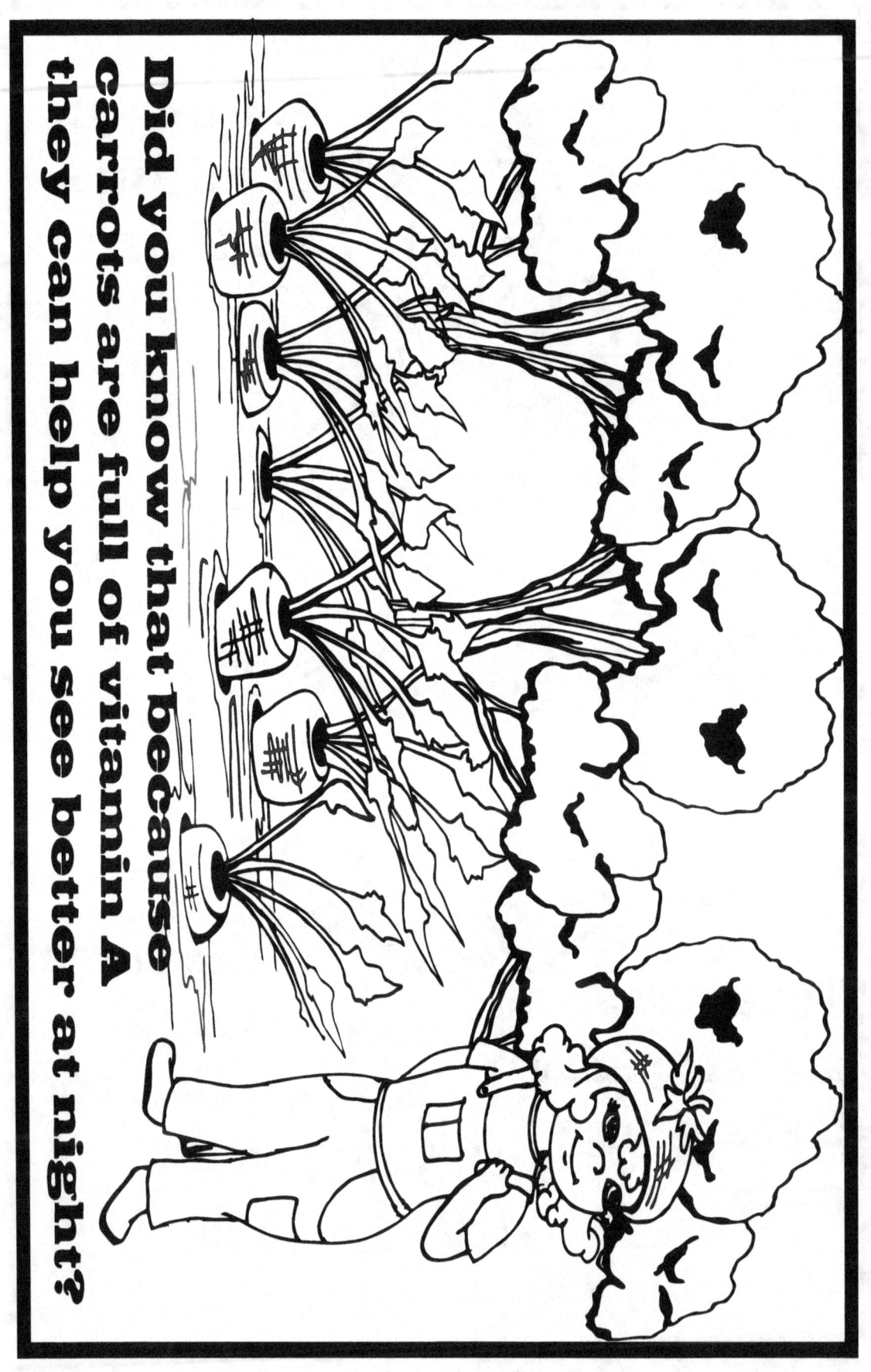

Did you know that because carrots are full of vitamin A they can help help you see better at night?

Until after WWI carrots were not widely popular with the people, however, they were brought to America in 1607

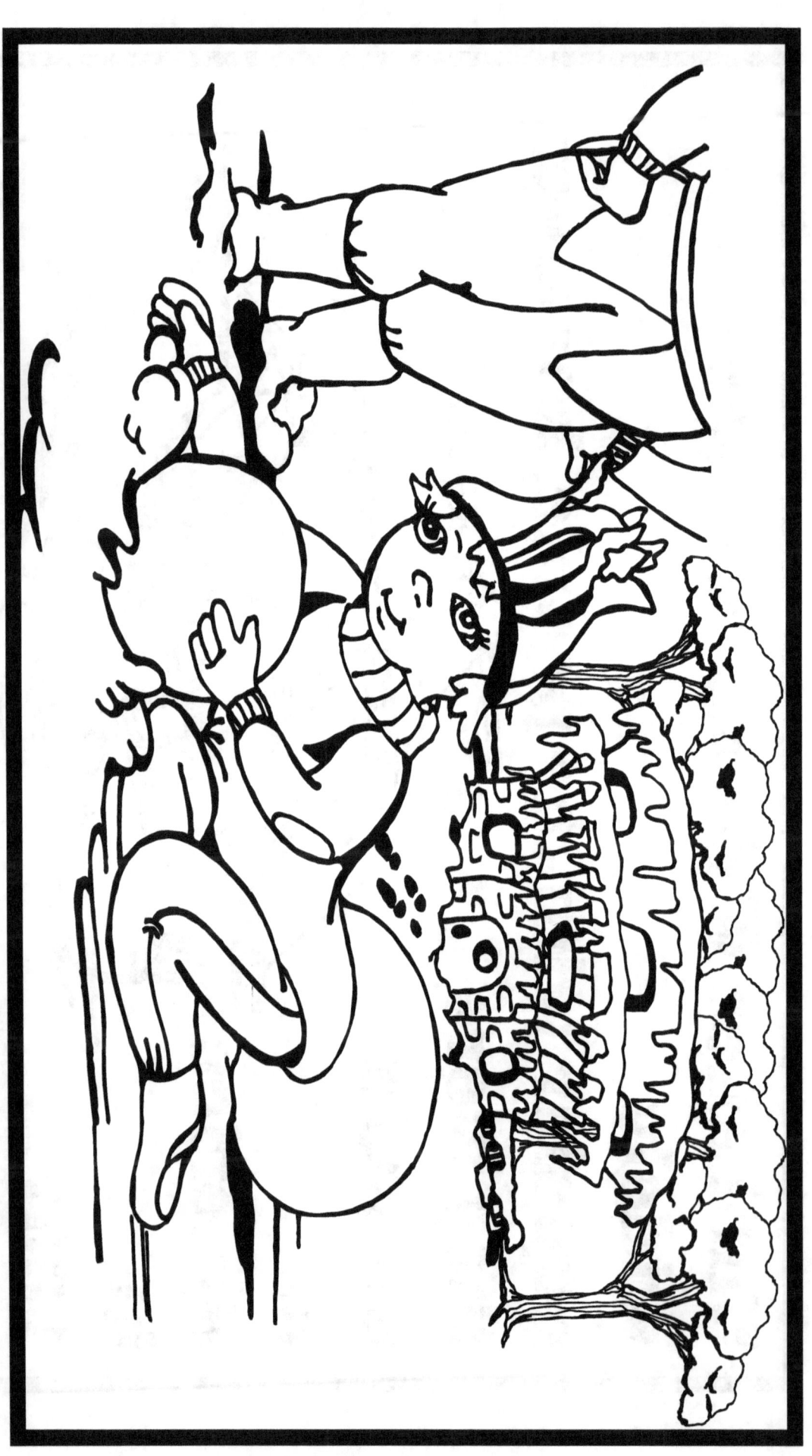

Portage, Michigan is home to the Celery Museum

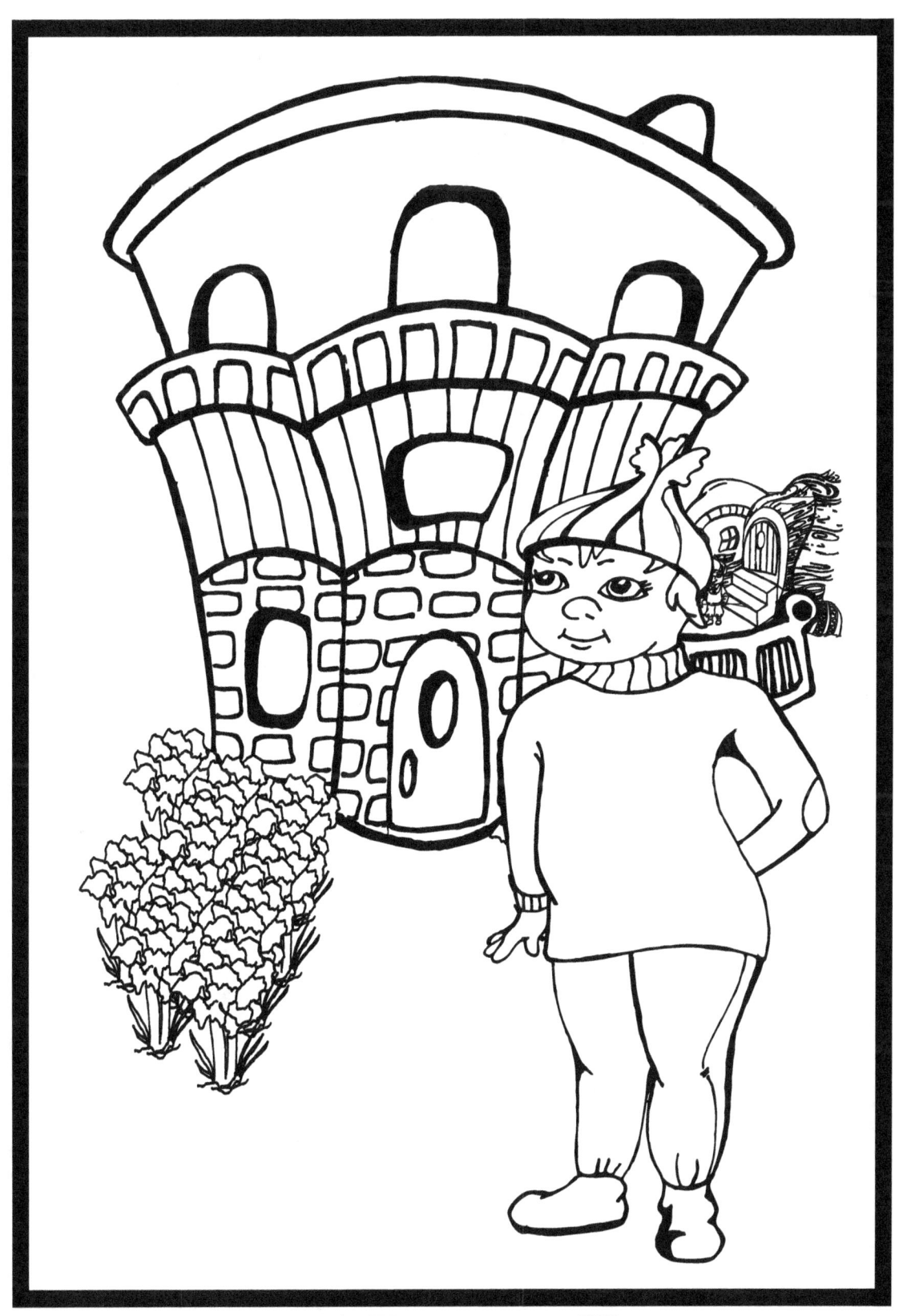

Celery and Peanut Butter, or celery and Ranch dressing is a healthy snack.

Celery originated in the Meditteranean and was used to flavor foods by the Romans and Greeks.

The Chinese used celery as a cure for many different physical ailments.

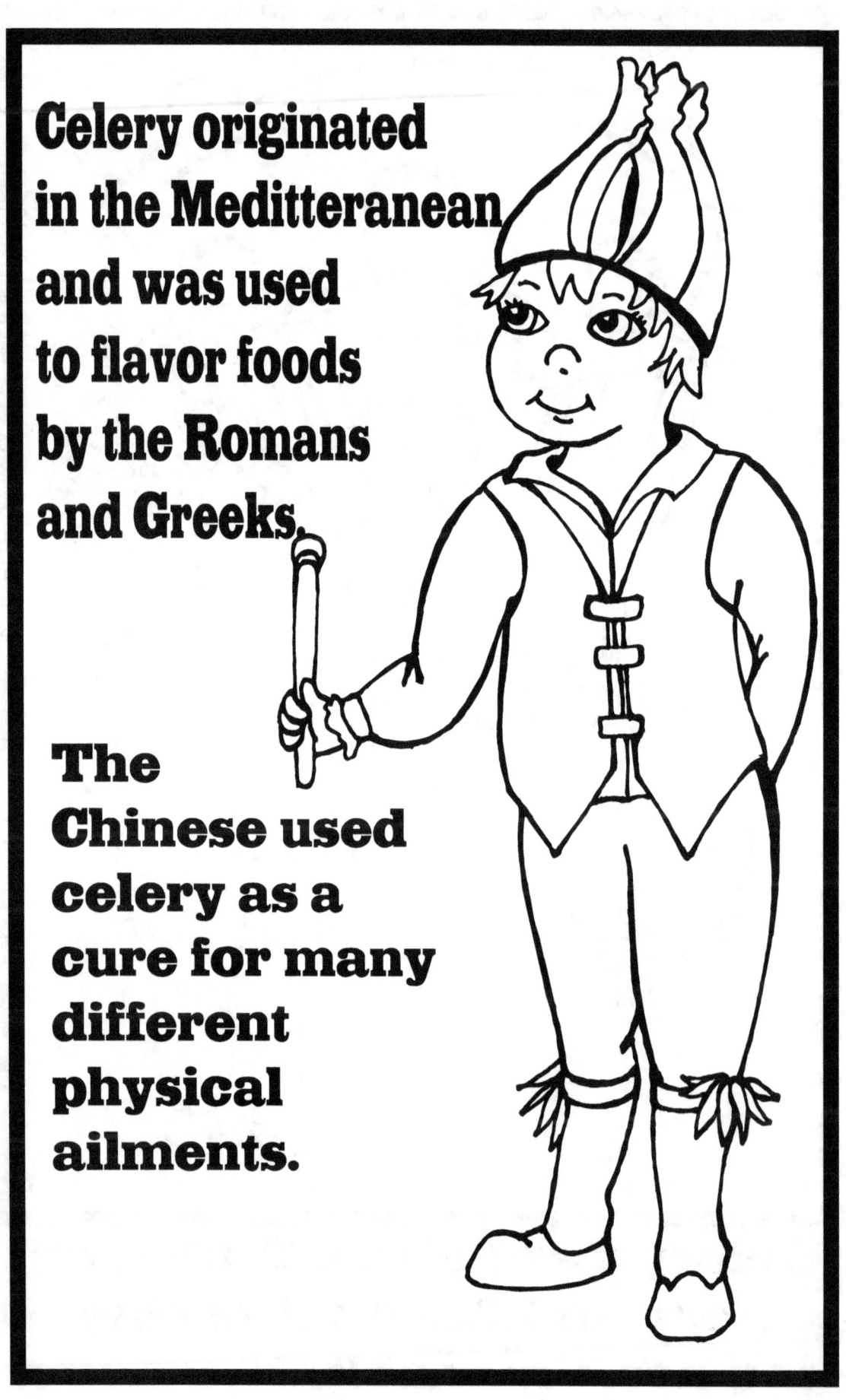

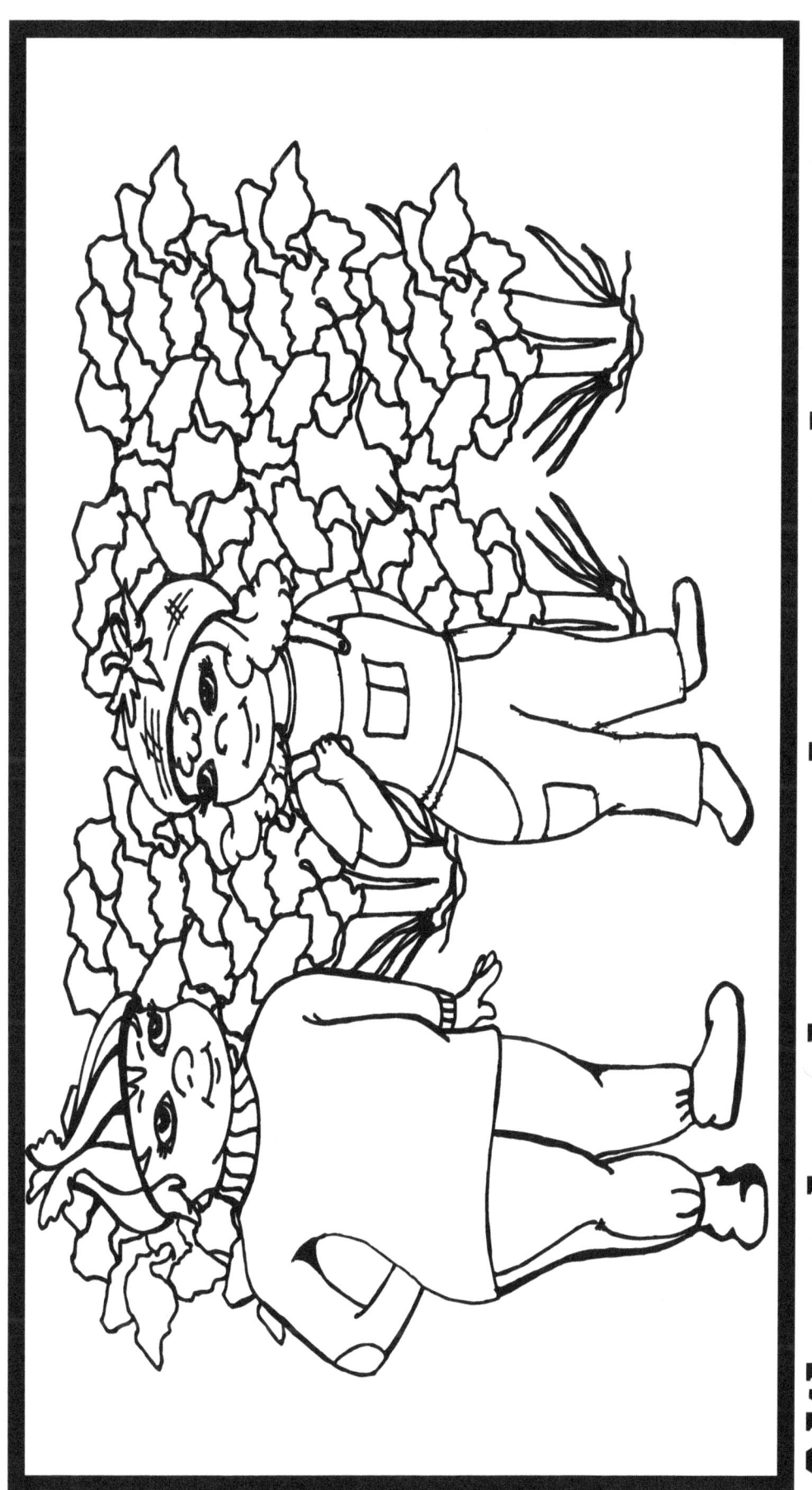

Although celery and carrots have many benefits in common, celery is the top of the plant and carrots are the root.

If you have 11 strawberries and you take three away, how many are left?

11 - 3 = _____

Hint: Color all but 3 stawberries to find the answer

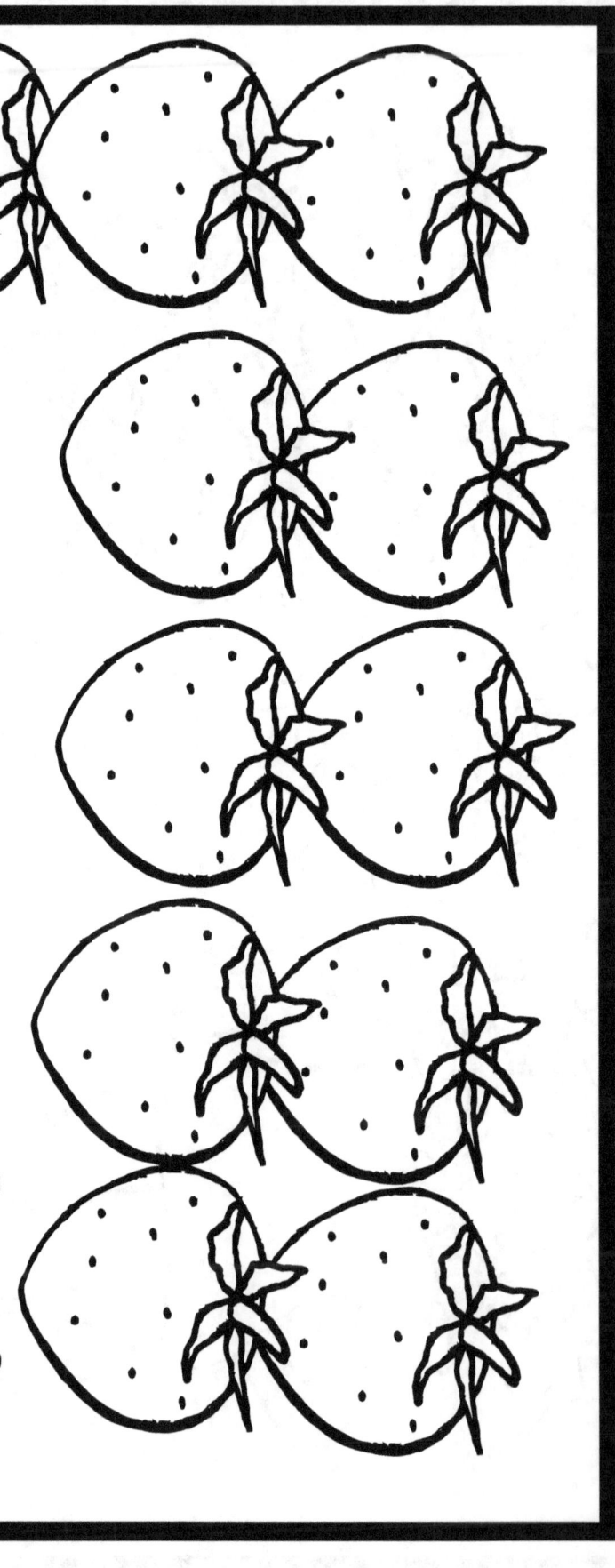

There are 11 Dances named for Foods:

1-The Mashed Potato
2-Peppermint Twist
3-Banana Split
4-Big Egg
5-Coffee Grind
6-Dipsey Doodle
7-Double Mint
8-The Fridge
9-The Honey Dipper
10-Snacky Poo
11-Turkey Trot

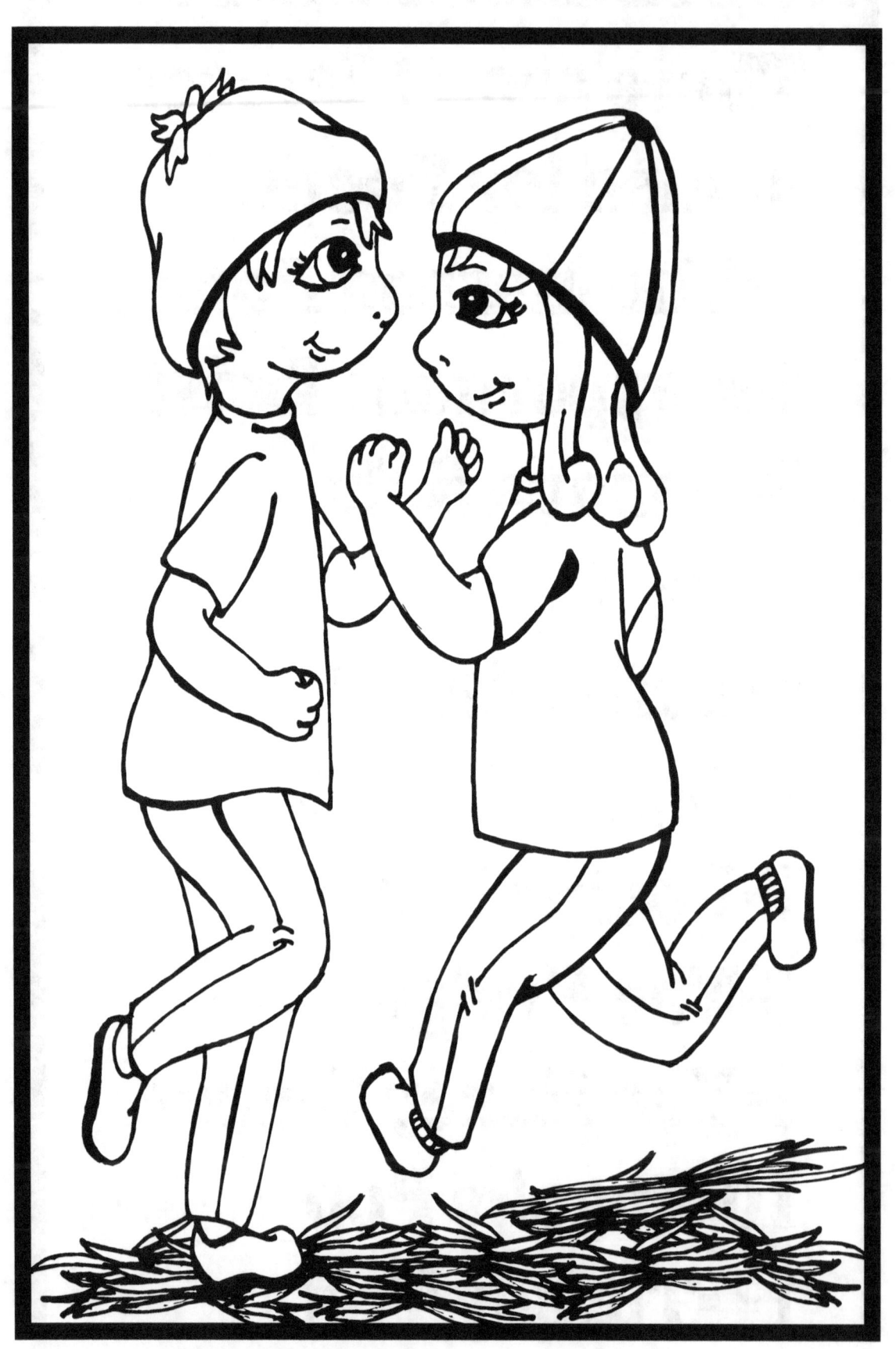

Peppermint Twist

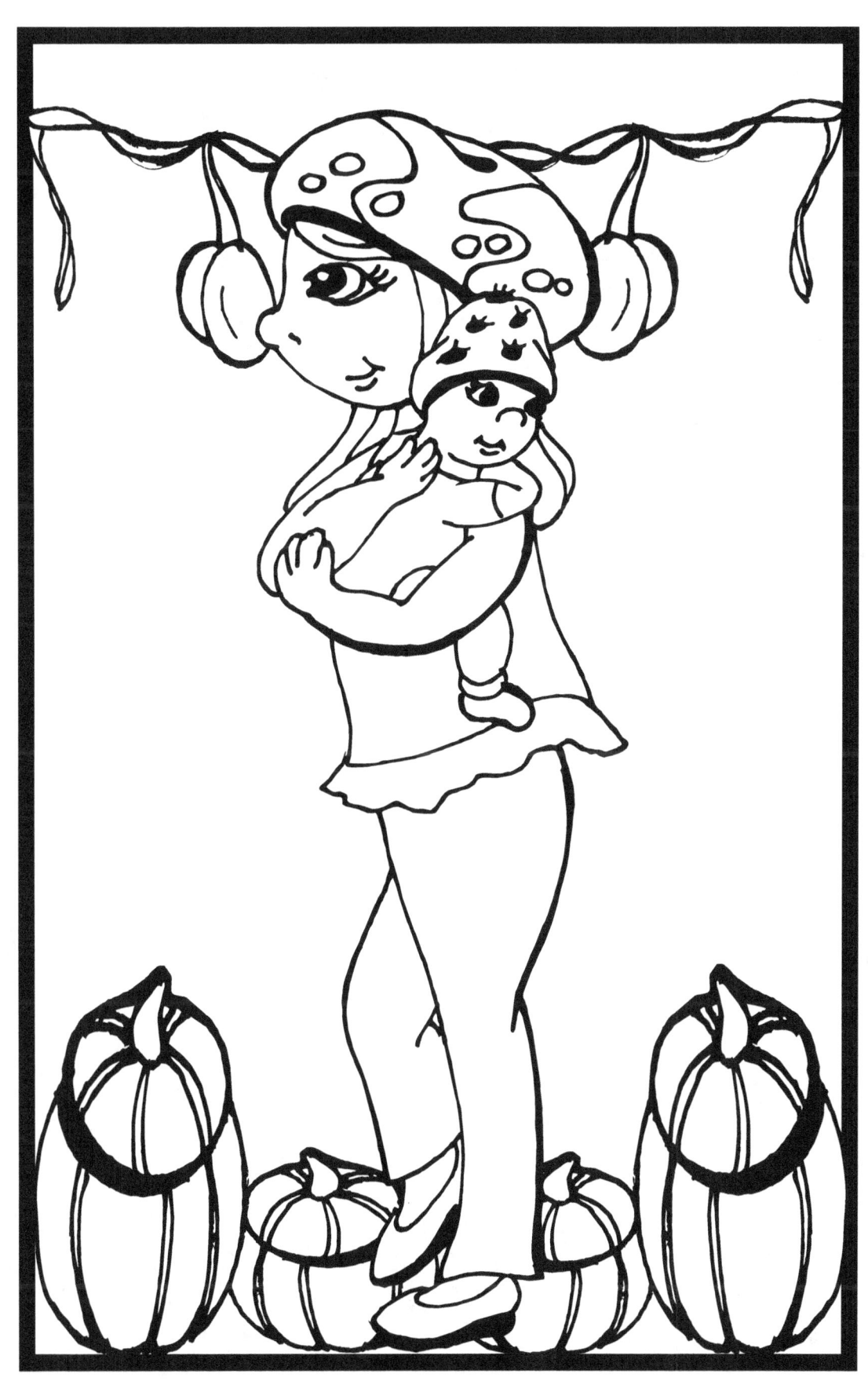

The Honey Dipper

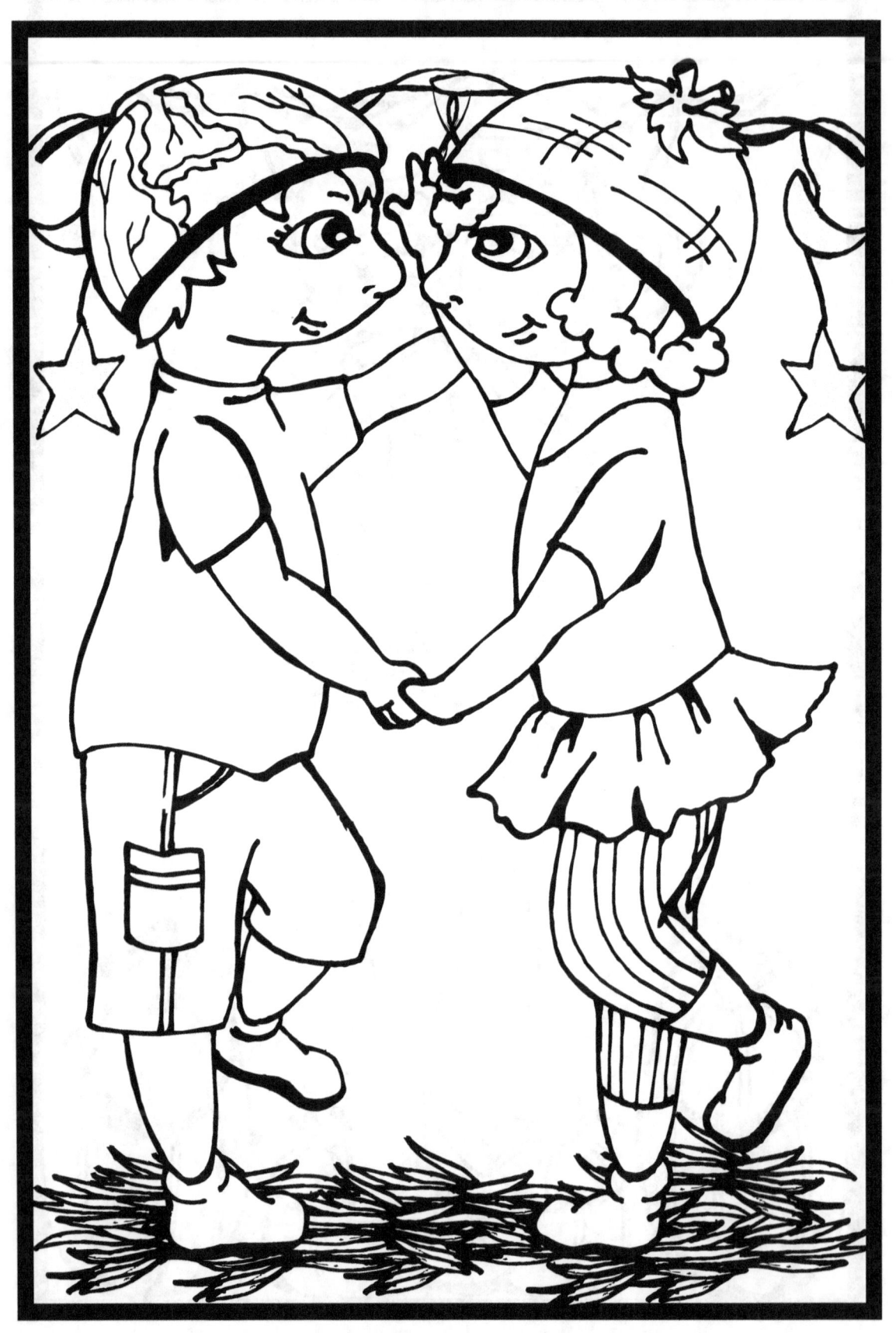

The Mashed Potato

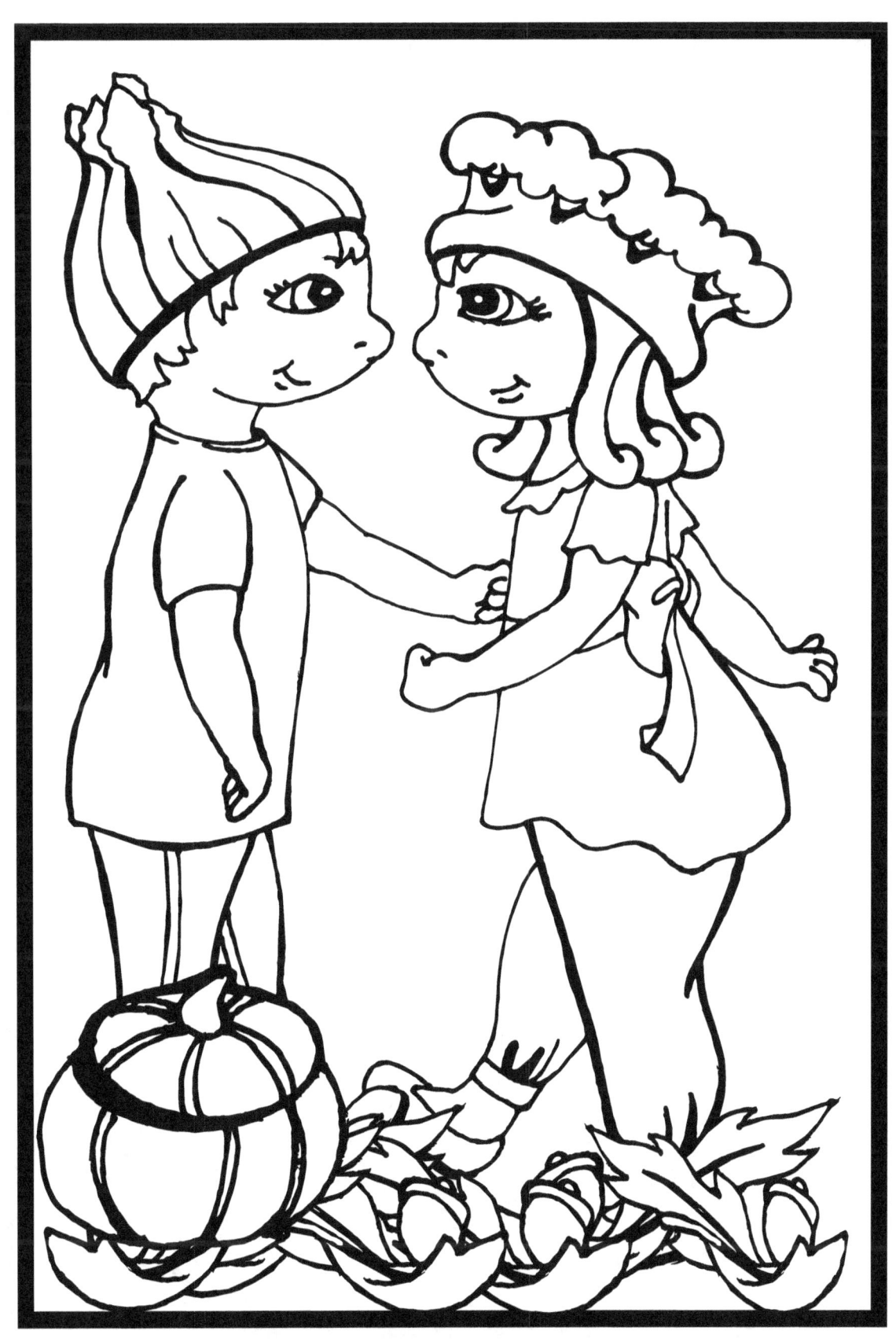

The Fridge

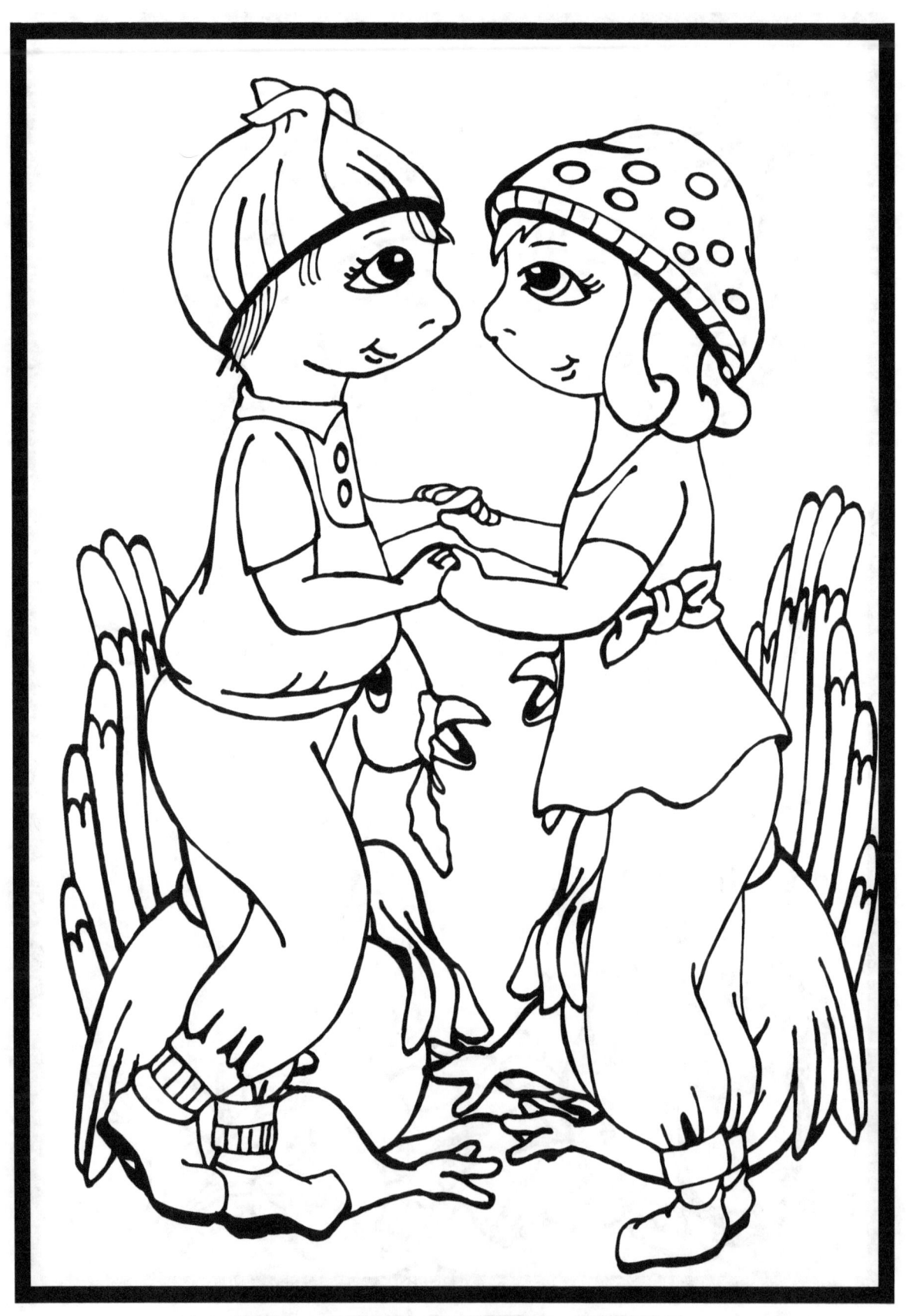

Turkey Trot

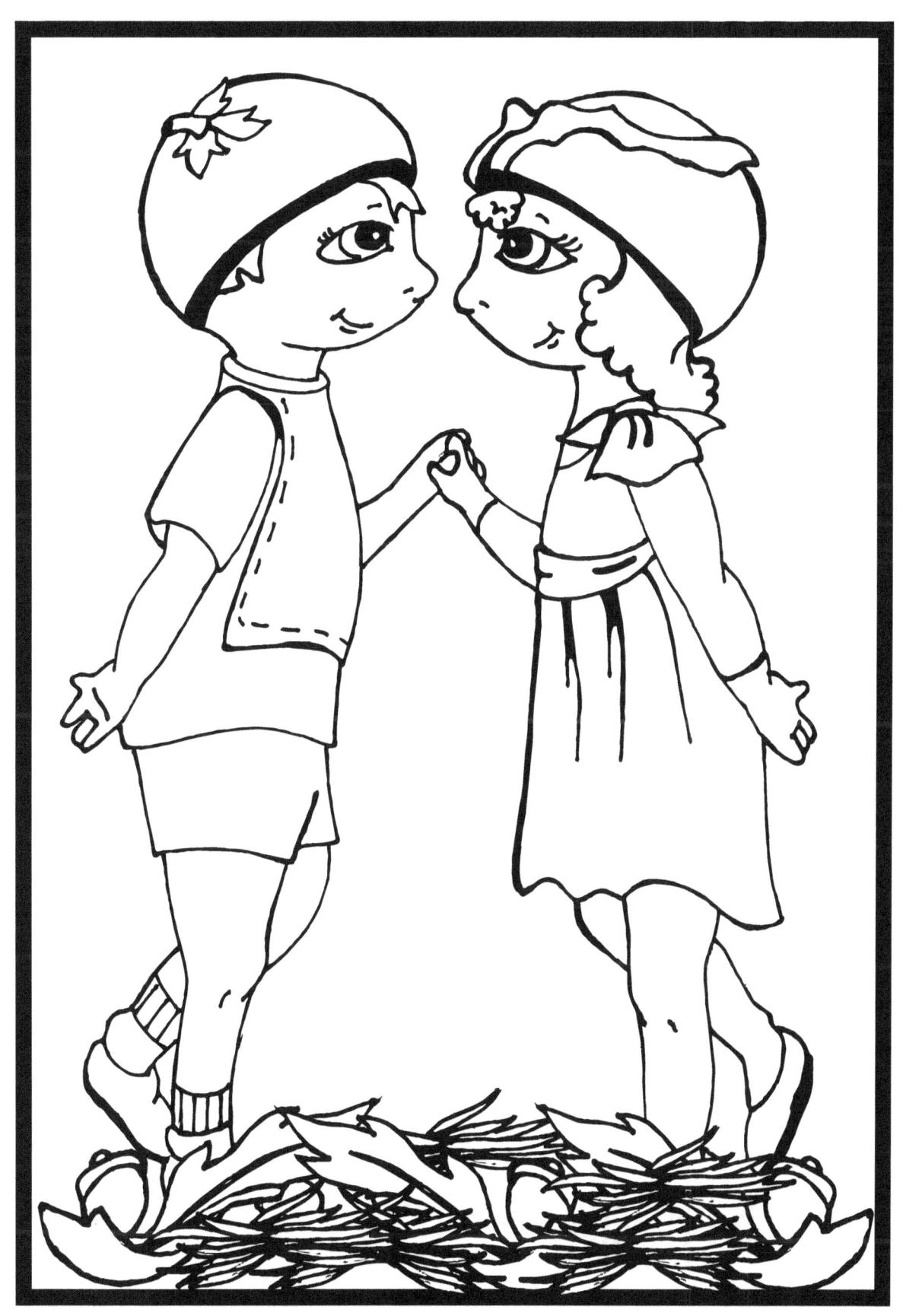

Snacky Poo

An apple in the
morning keeps
the doctor
awake.

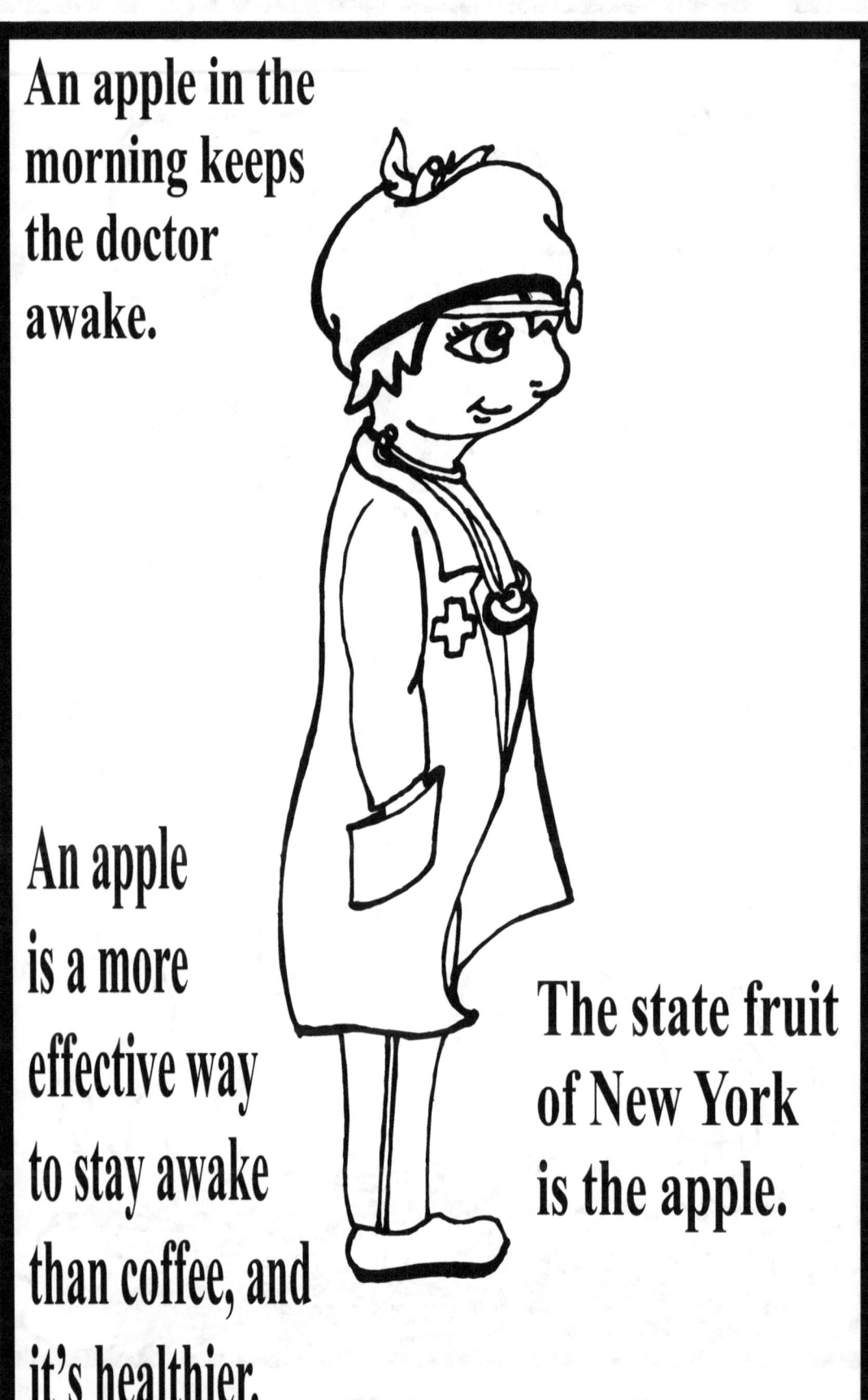

An apple
is a more
effective way
to stay awake
than coffee, and
it's healthier.

The state fruit
of New York
is the apple.

EGG FOO YUNG BEHIND THE REFRIGERATOR

When my children were small, getting two of them
to eat anything that didn't start with ham and end
with burger was difficult. Tristan
and Bryan lee wouldn't
eat anything and they hated vegetables.
The "Try it before you say you don't like it" thing didn't
work. They would sit for hours staring at their plates
until they fell asleep.
One night I fixed egg foo yung and they sat, and sat,
and sat staring at their plates. Finally, I went back
into the kitchen to find both plates empty. I was so
proud...well, for almost two weeks until I found
the egg foo yung behind the refrigerator.

Children will eat foods they don't
like, if you make it fun for them.

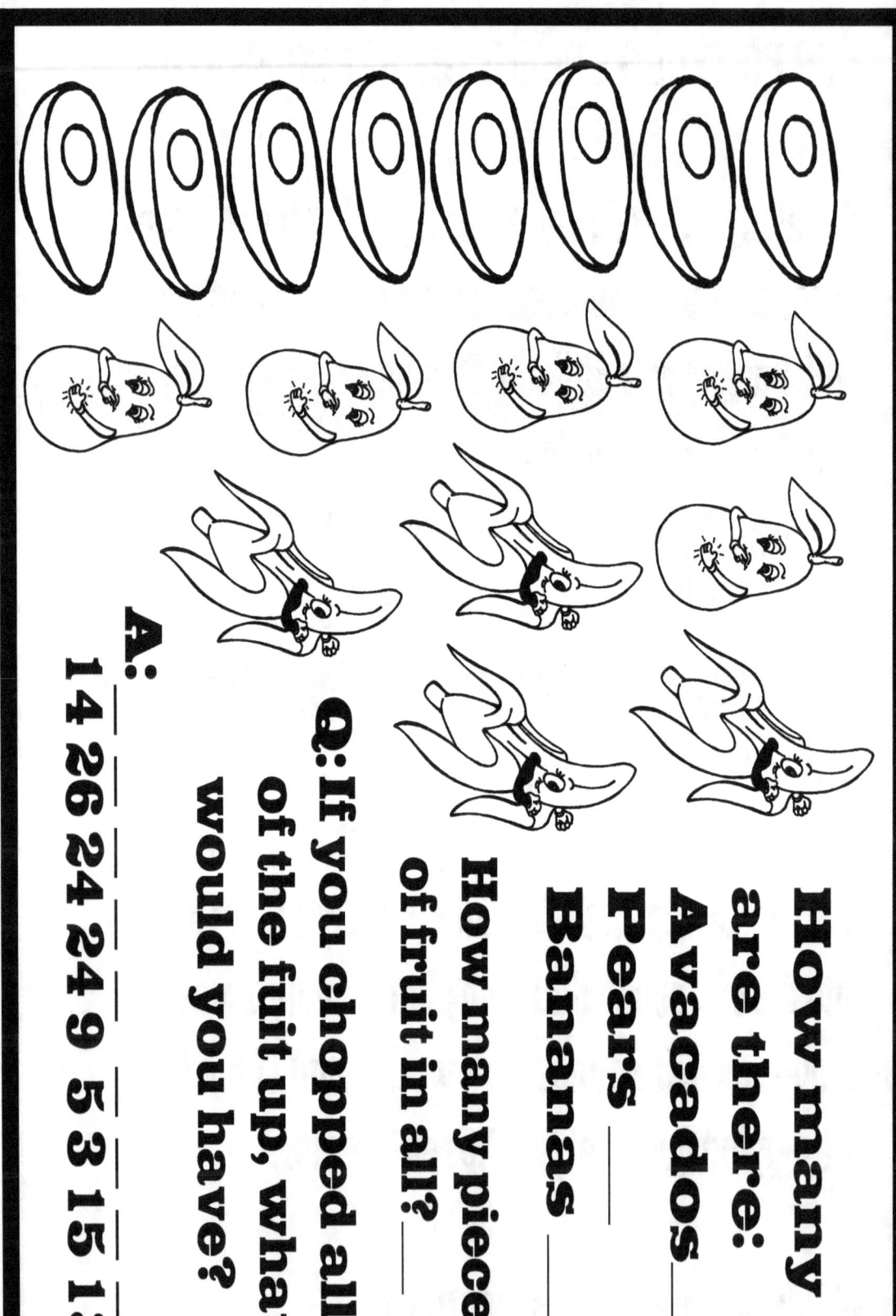

How many are there:

Avacados ____

Pears ____

Bananas ____

How many pieces of fruit in all? ____

Q: If you chopped all of the fuit up, what would you have?

A: __ __ __ __ __ __ __

14 26 24 9 5 3 15 13

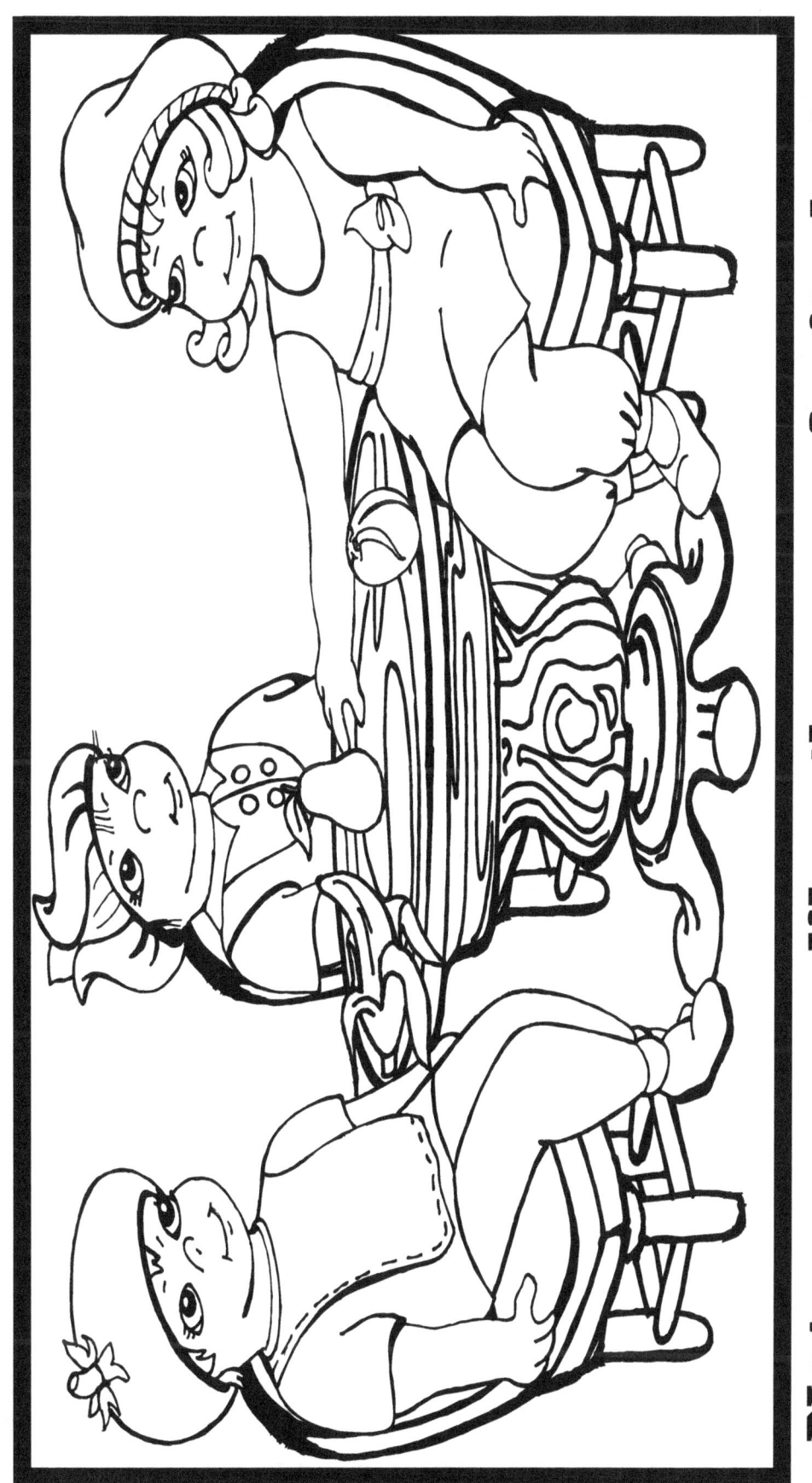

Not everyone likes the same fruits, but all fruits are rich in vitamins and good for you.

Fruit and Vegetable websites:

1: www.livestrong.com

2: www.whfood.com

3: http://www.kids-cooking-activities.com/

There are many sources for trivia and history on the internet, as well.

True or False

Avacados are both a fruit and a vegetable? ____

Zucchini is 95% water? ____

Watermelon and Pumkin belong to the same family? ____

The tomato was declared a vegetable by the Supreme Court? ____

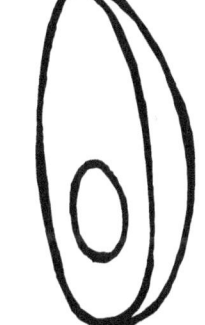
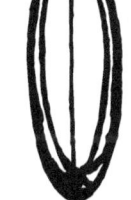
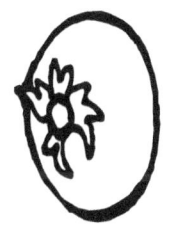

Hippocrates "The Father of Western Medicine" believed that Garlic had many curative properties.

Among these were the treatment of parasites, respiratory ailments, indegestion, and fatigue. Though some studies have proven that garlic is not a cure-all, it is still beneficial for many diseases and illnesses.

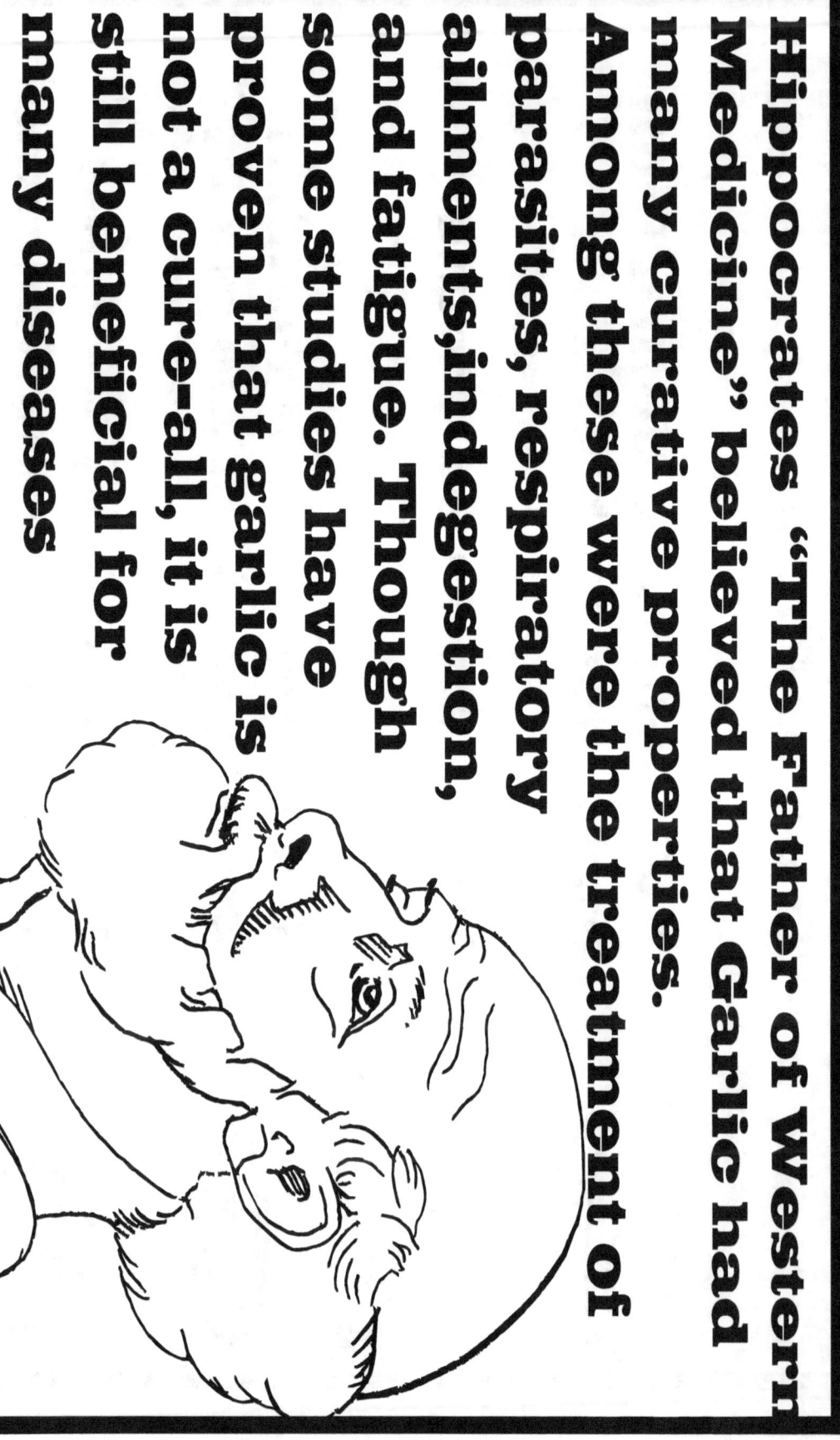

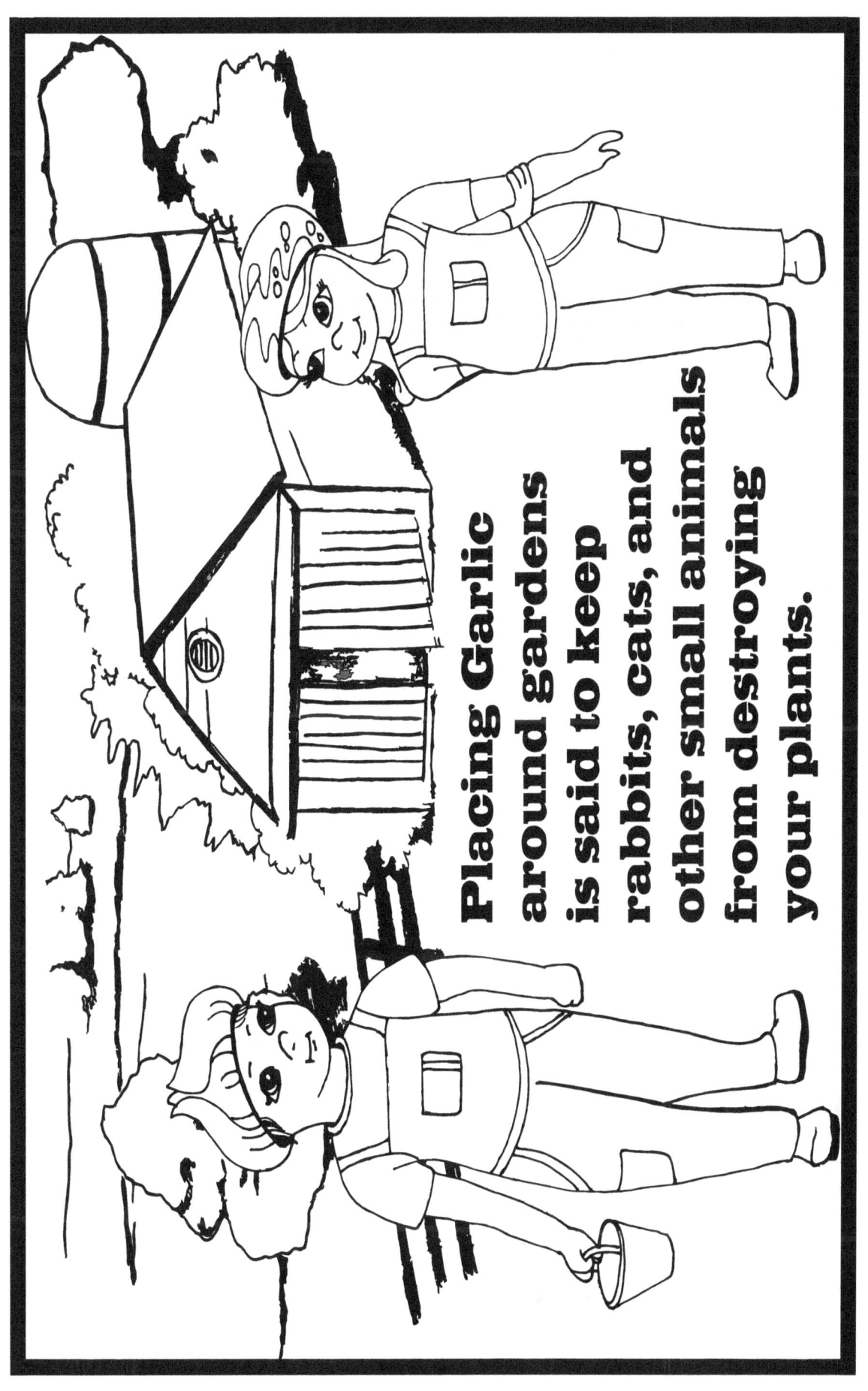

Placing Garlic around gardens is said to keep rabbits, cats, and other small animals from destroying your plants.

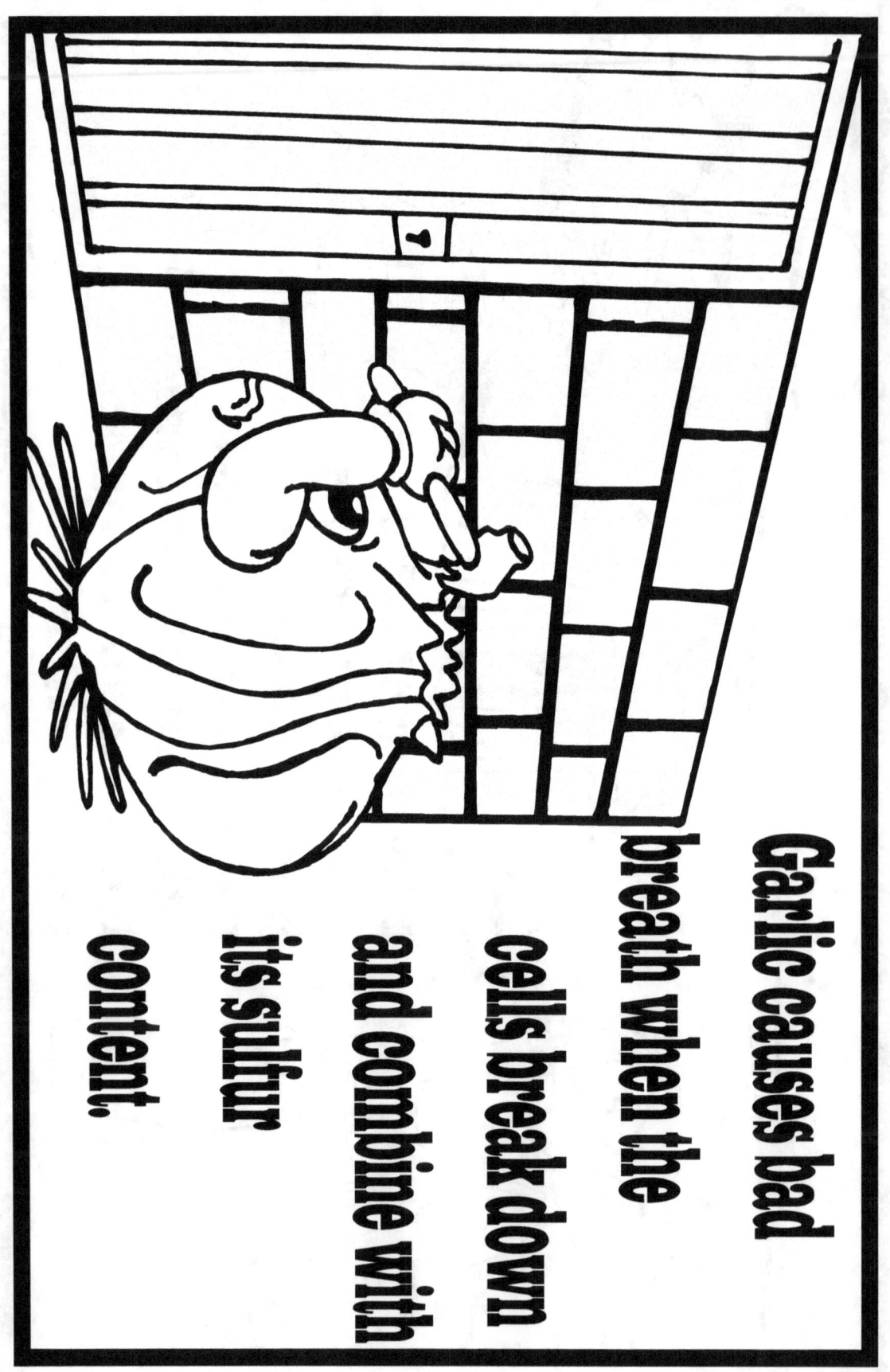

Garlic causes bad breath when the cells break down and combine with its sulfur content.

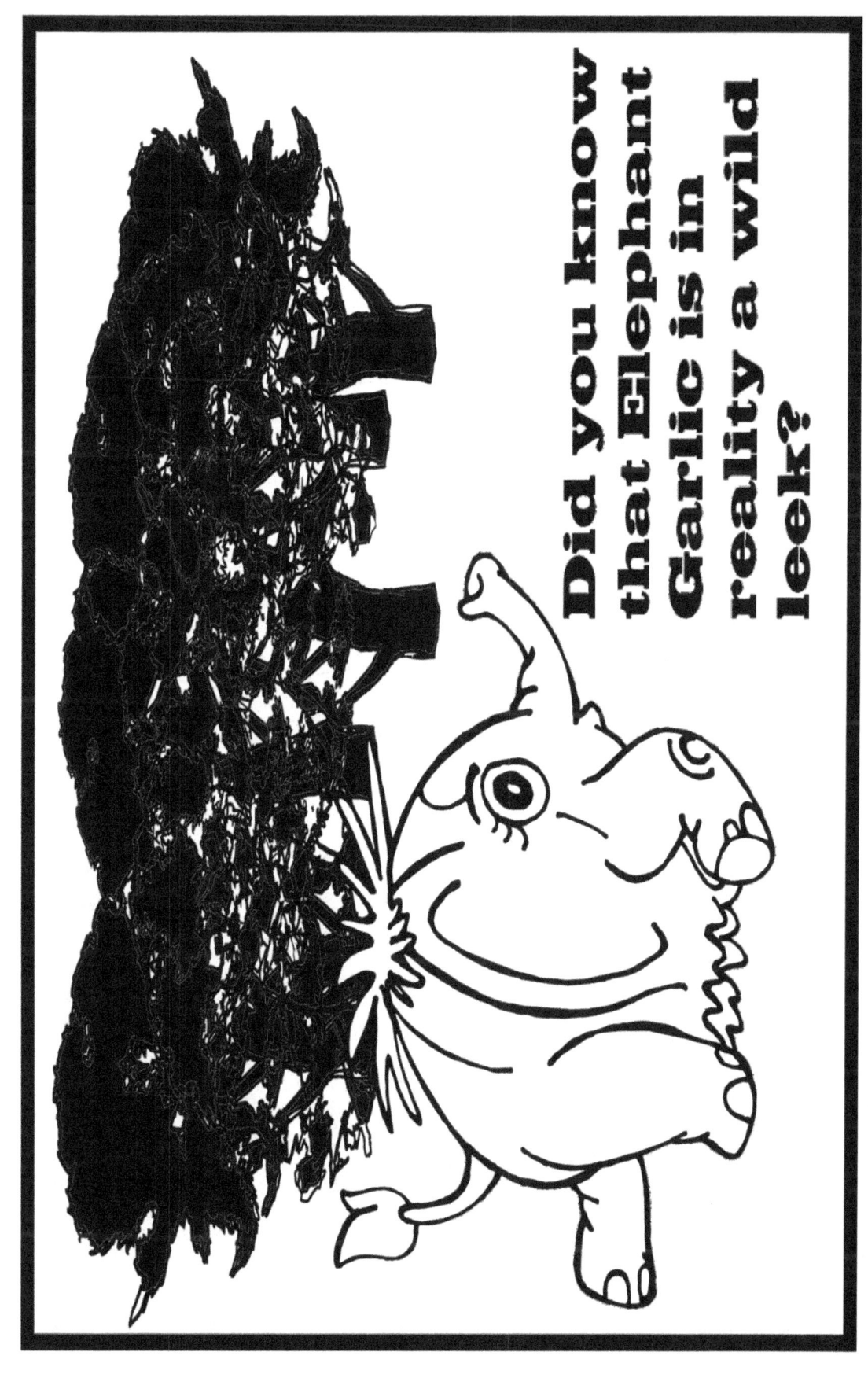

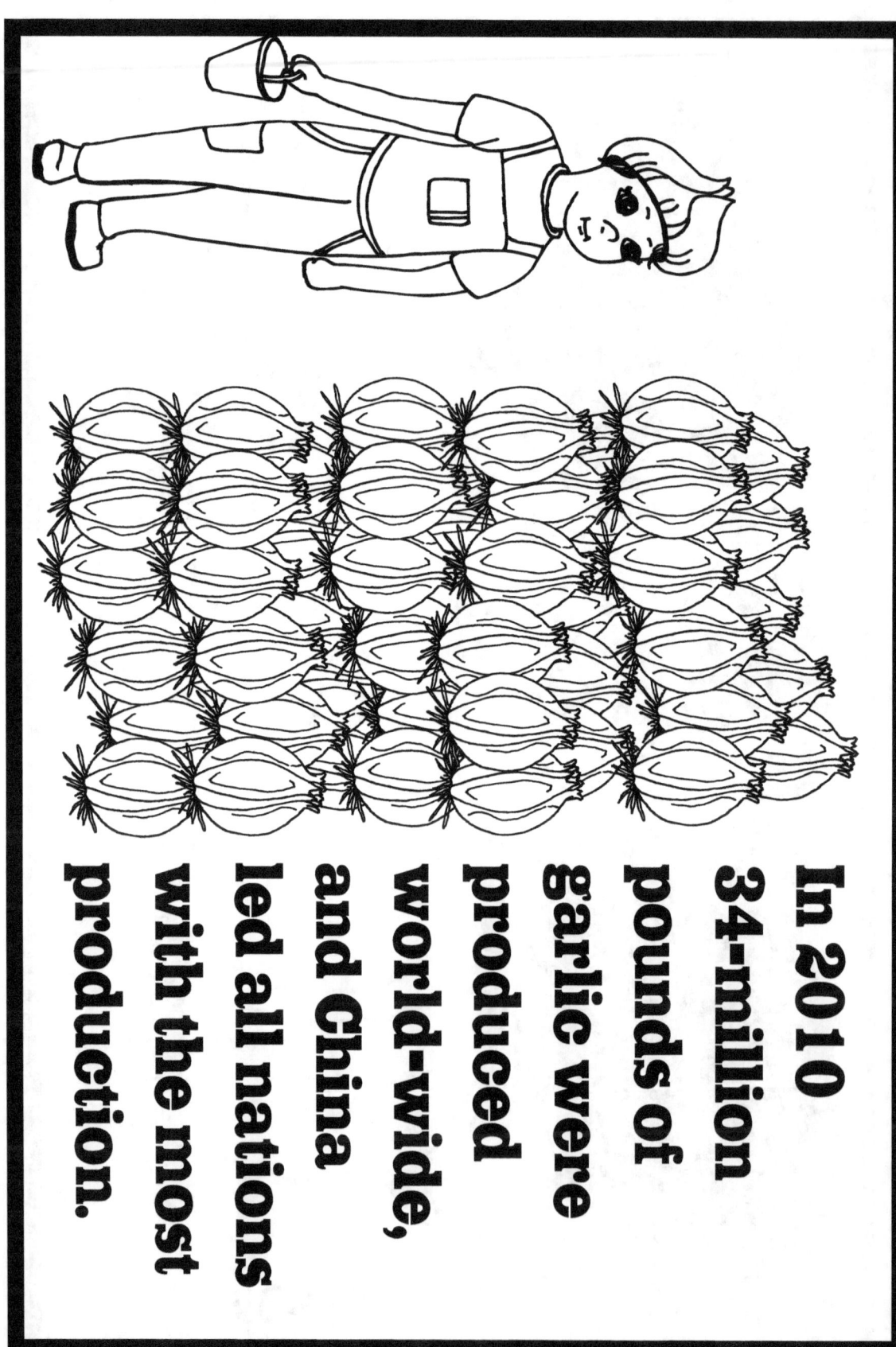

In 2010
34-million
pounds of
garlic were
produced
world-wide,
and China
led all nations
with the most
production.

During WWI and WWII, garlic was used as an antiseptic to treat gangrene.

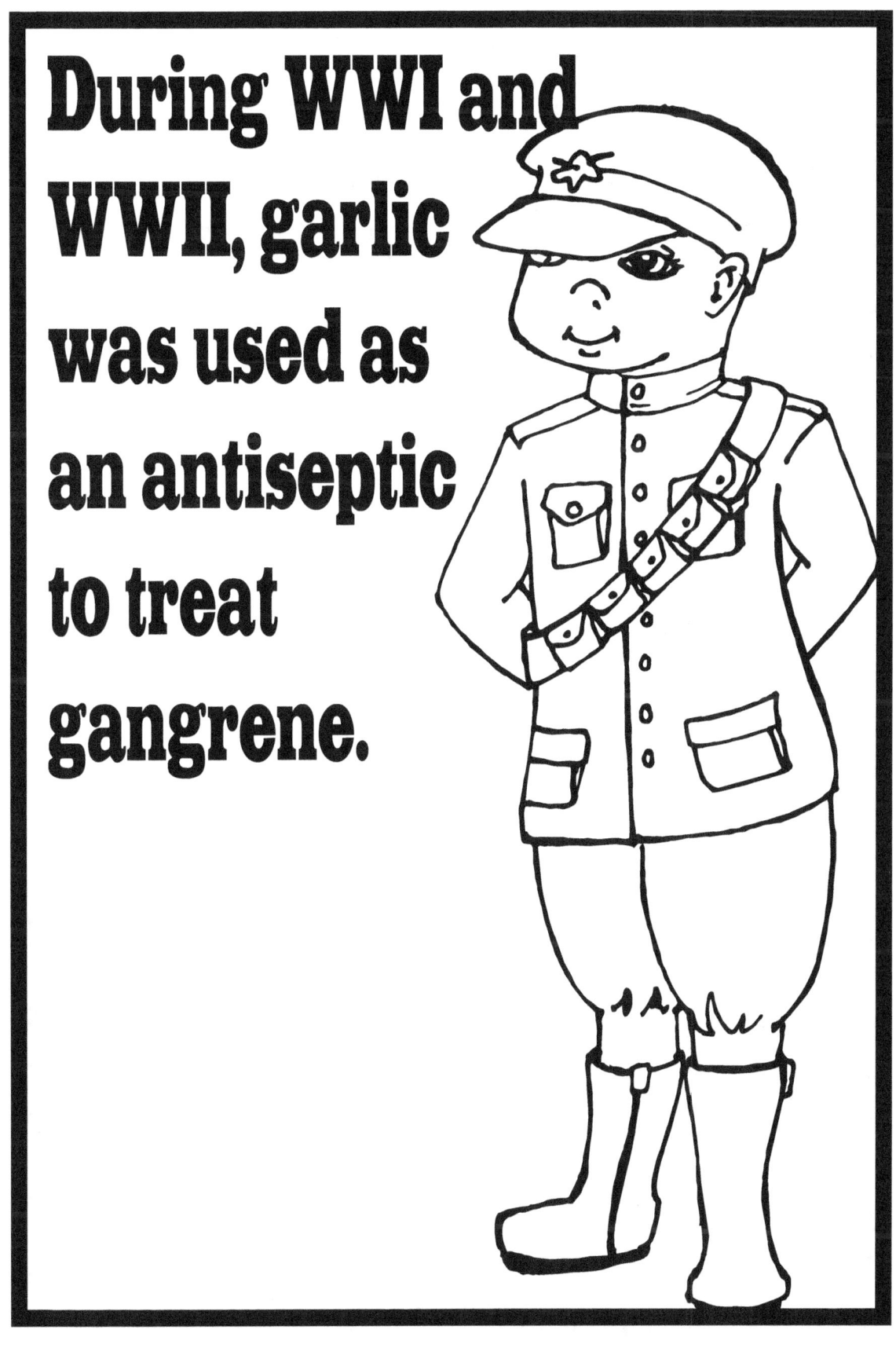

In days of old, many country folk thought that garlic possessed magic powers and would ward off evil spirits, demons, vampires, werewolves and witches.

Drinking milk has proven to make your breath less-stinky when eating garlic.

Named Lactuca by the Romans, lettuce was first grown in 2680 BC by the Egyptians. They domesticated the plant for its seeds and oil.

The Vitamins in Lettuce:

A
B1
B2
B5
B6
B9
C
E
K

The Minerals:

Calcium
Iron
Magnesium
Manganese
Phosphorus
Potassium
Sodium
Zinc

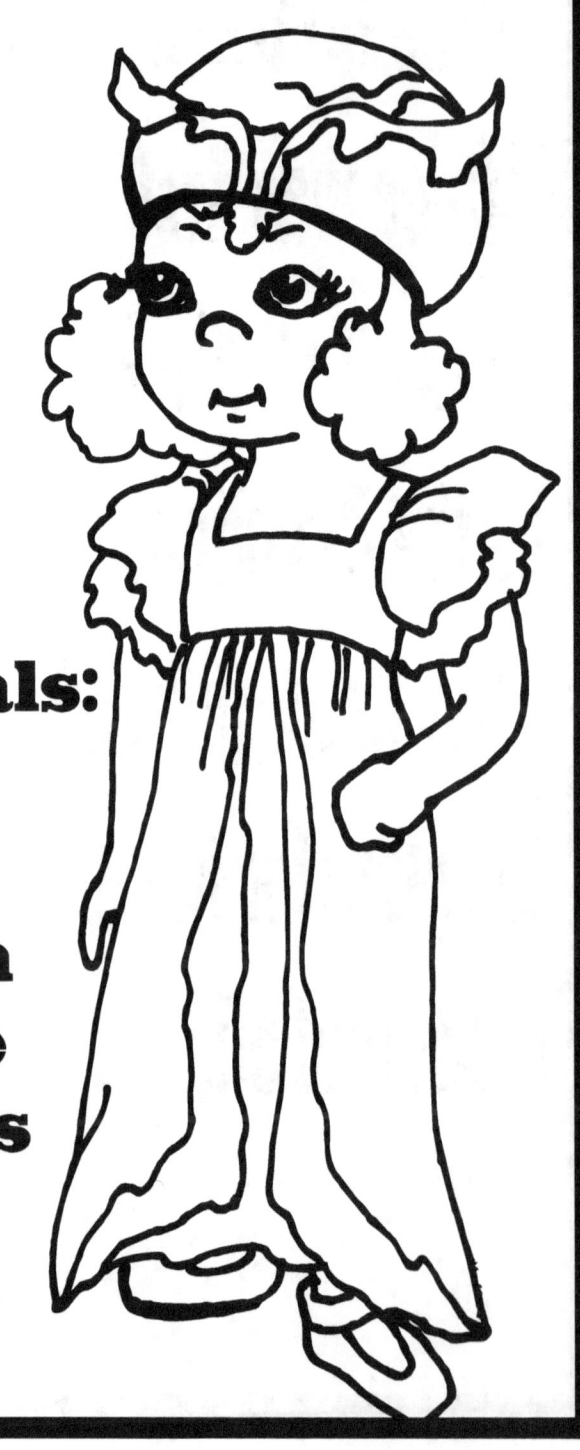

Mirepoix (carrots, celery, and onions) is the basis for most soups and sauces.

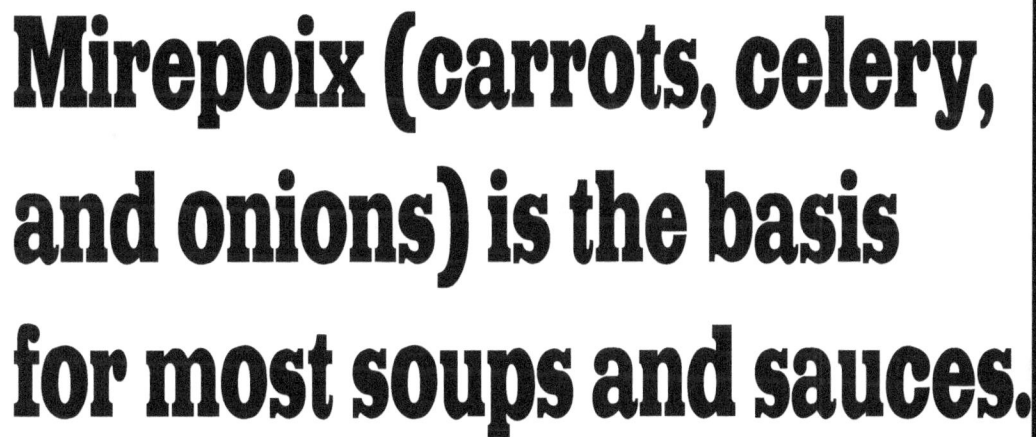

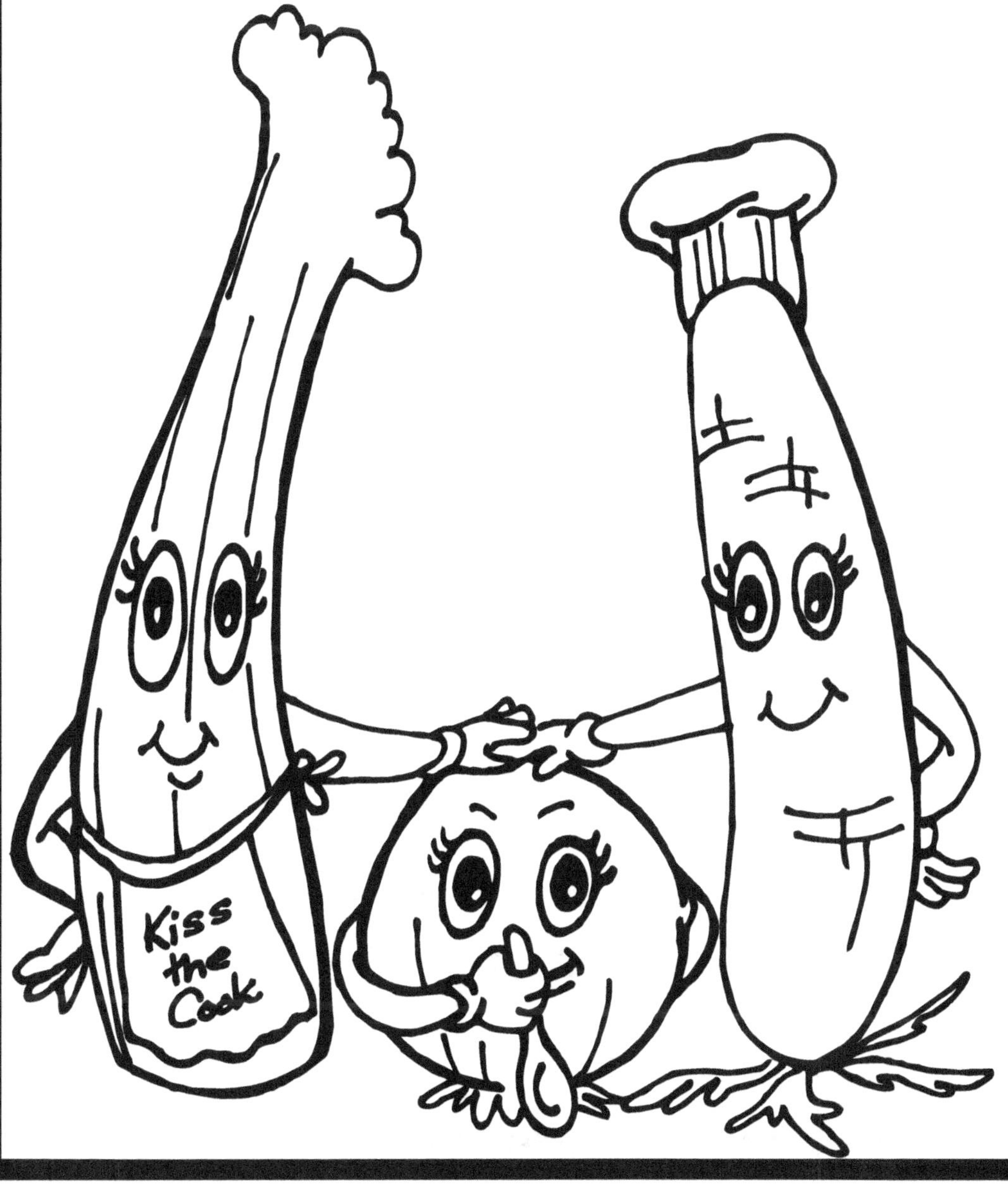

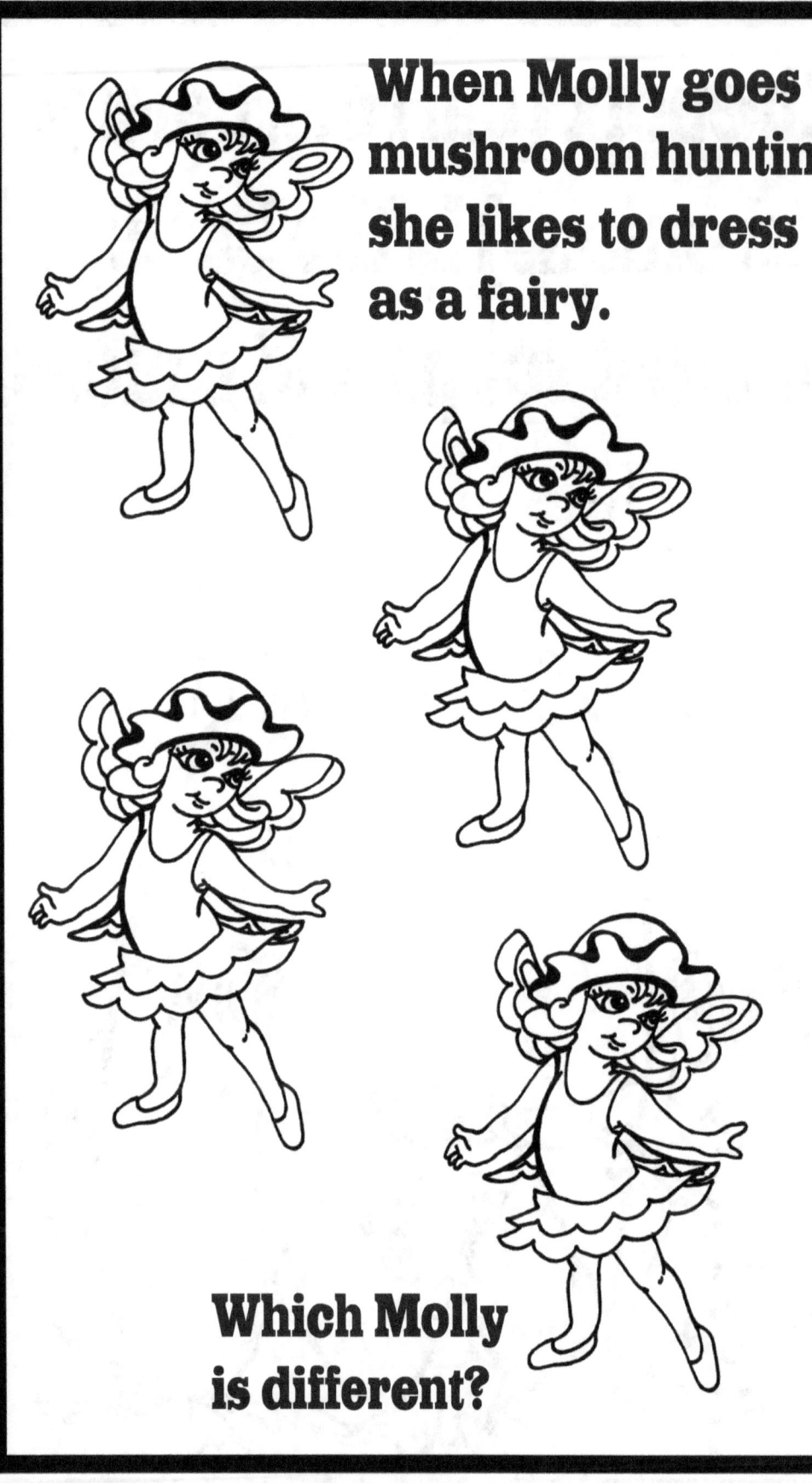

When Molly goes mushroom hunting she likes to dress as a fairy.

Which Molly is different?

Help Molly find the mushrooms.

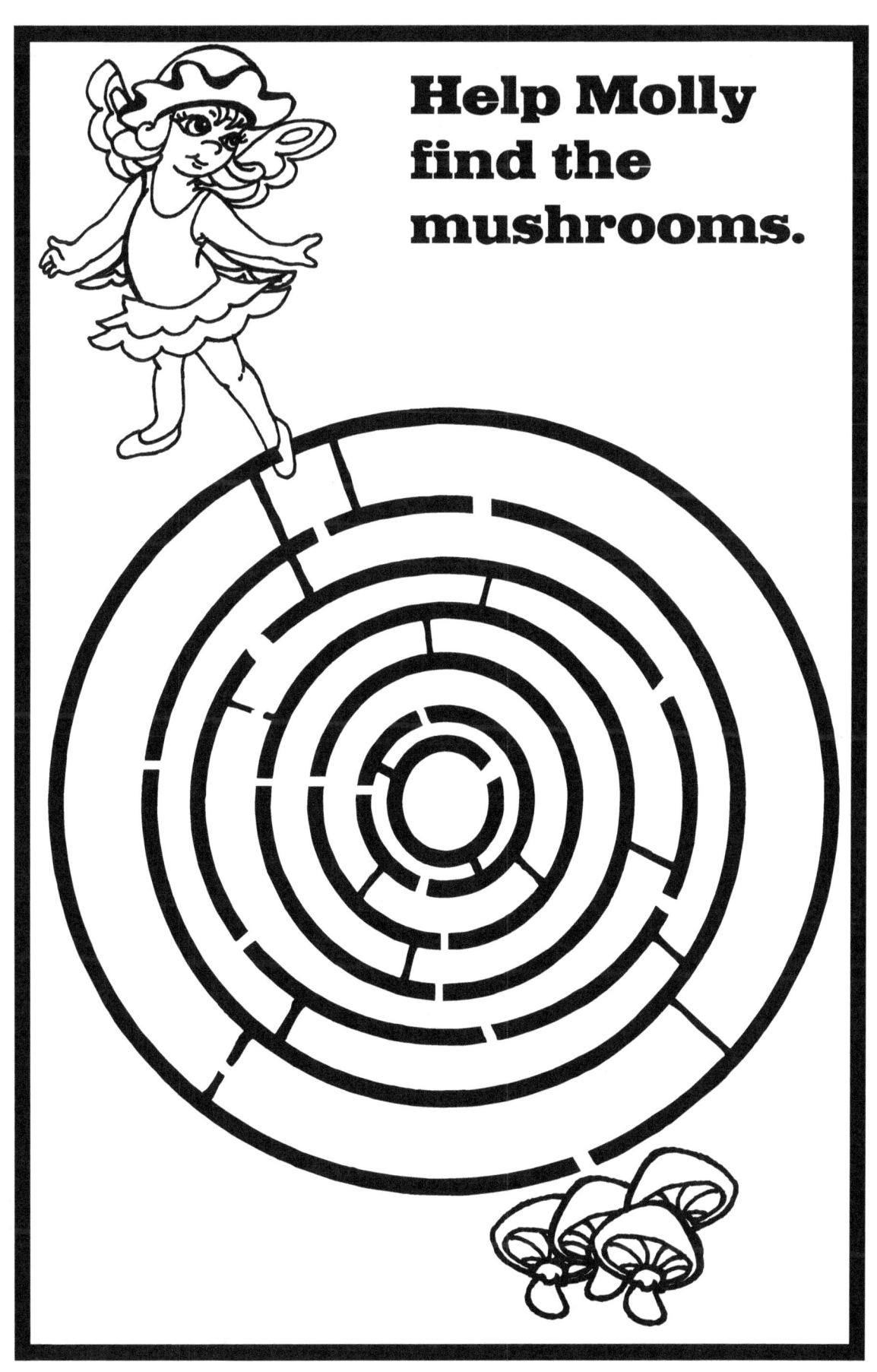

Mycoloist study mushrooms.

Mycophagists hunt mushrooms.

Both know the difference between

a poisonous mushroom and an

edible mushroom.

The spores (seeds)

of the mushroom

can be found on their

gills.

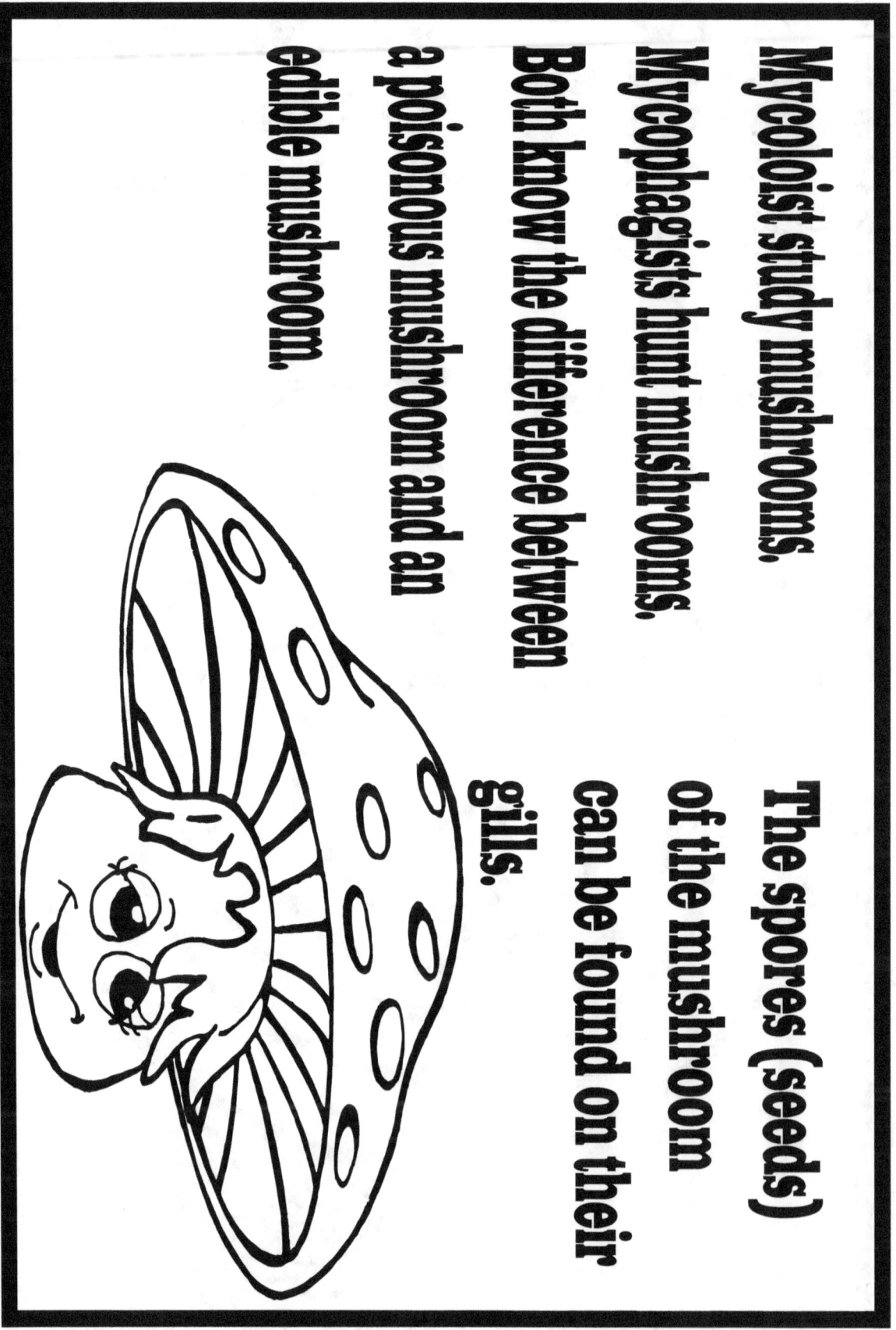

Encompassing 14,000 species, the mushroom is known as the "meat" of the vegetable world.

Mushrooms and their extracts are being studied as use in many fields of medicine.

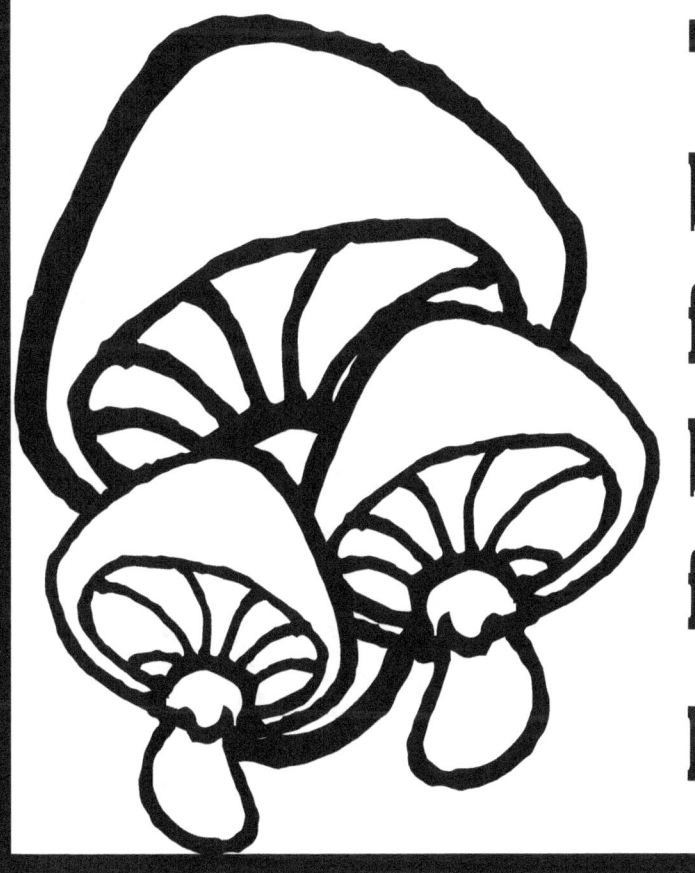

They have been used for centuries by the Chinese for medicinal purposes

Sliced mushrooms and diced onions and garlic are the mirepoix of sauces and gravies for meats such as steak! The mushrooms spongy consistency makes it a good choice for sauces, soups, and casseroles.

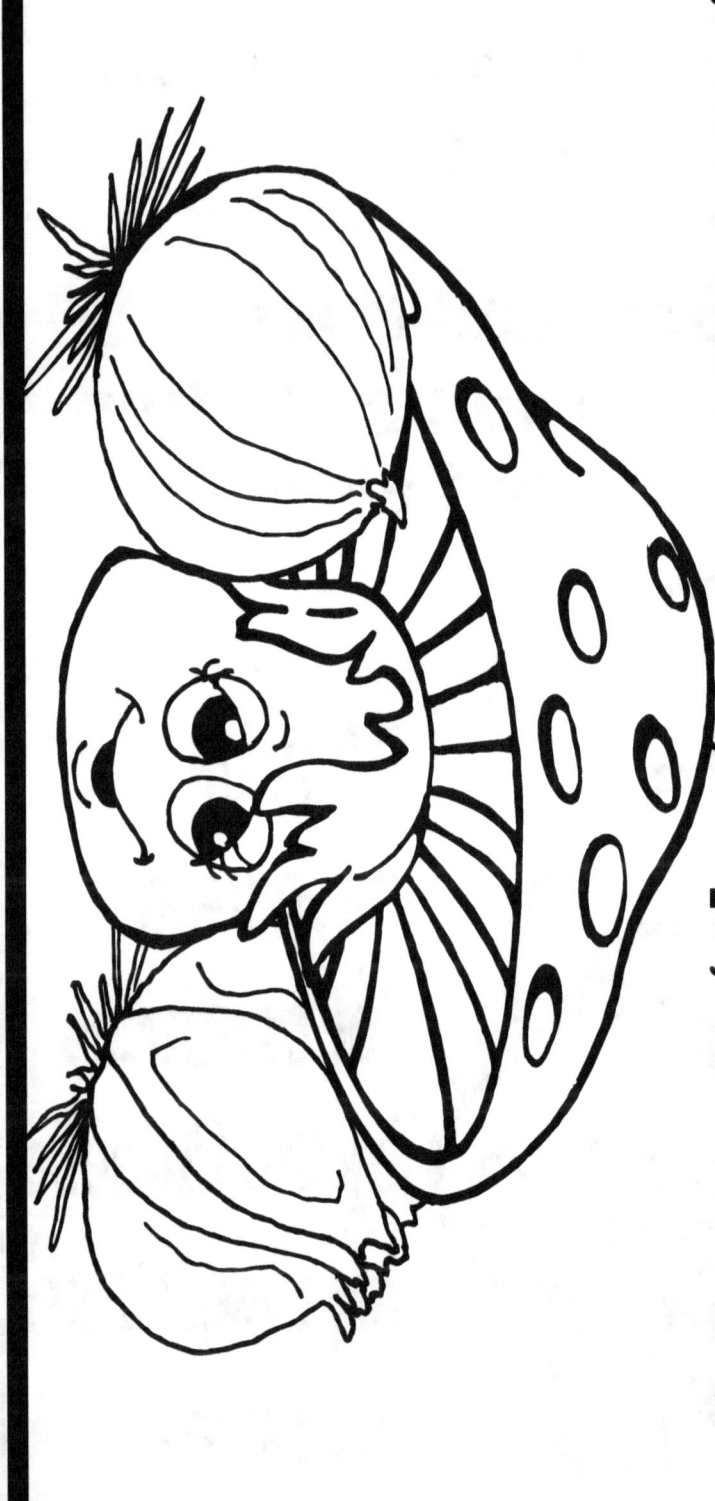

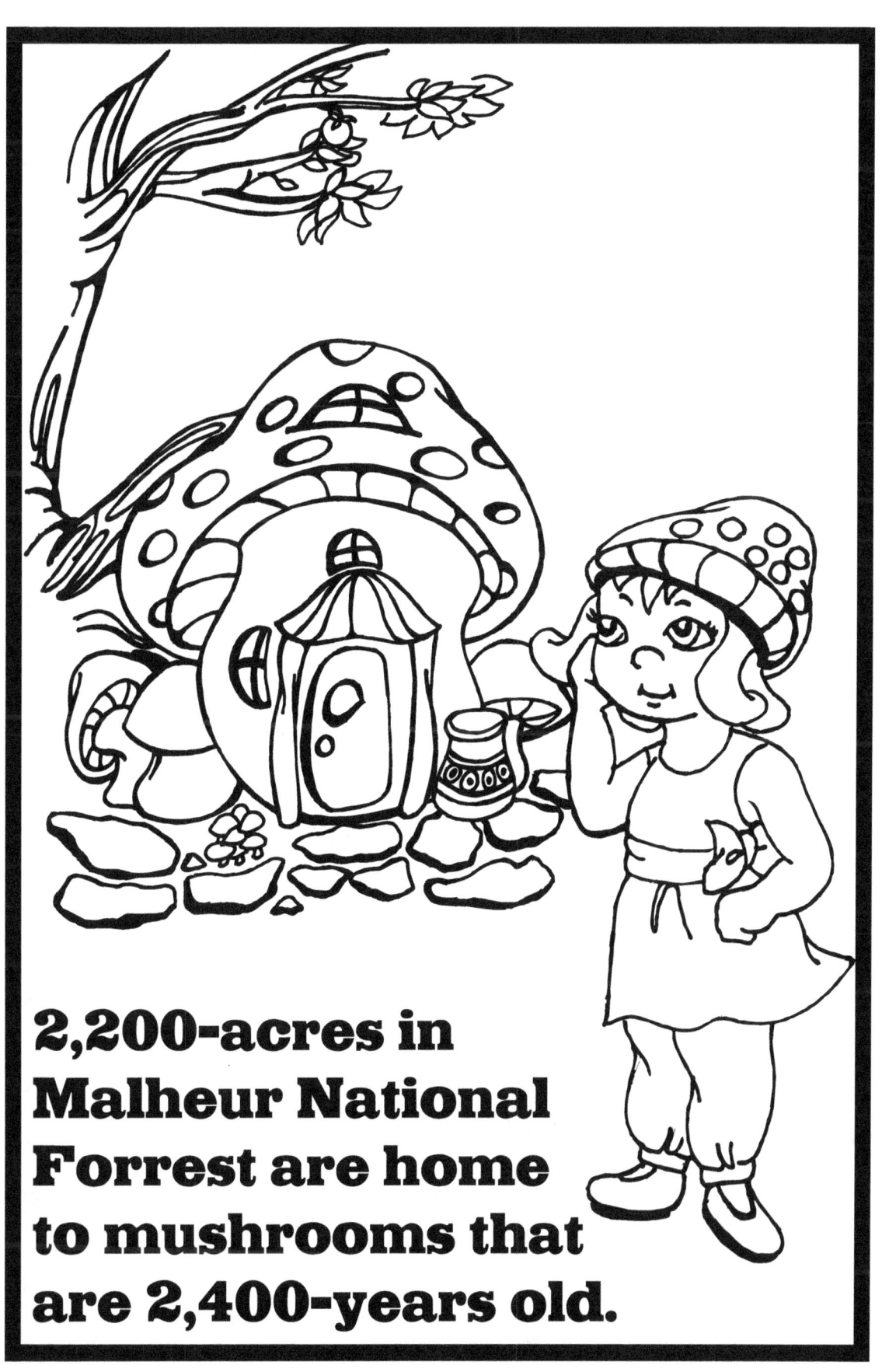

2,200-acres in Malheur National Forrest are home to mushrooms that are 2,400-years old.

Websites for more information

1: www.oddee.com/item_96650.aspx
10 largest fruits and vegetables

2:www.networx.com/article/the-worlds-biggest-vegetables

3:www.carrotmuseum.co.uk/record.html

John Evans-Guiness Book of Records

4:www.dailymail.co.uk/news/article-2038439/Pensioner-Peter-Glazebrook-grows-worlds-biggest-onion.html

5:http://gardening.about.com/od/vegetables/a/Giant-Vegetables.htm

6:www.gardenersnet.com/vegetable/giants.htm

7: www.recordholders.org/en/records/vegetables2.thml

8:www.worldsbiggest.com/2010/03/worlds-biggest-foods.html

9:http://gadling.com/2007/07/16/giant-mutant-like-vegetables-at-alaska-state-fair/

Onions strengthen your immune system to help you feel well.

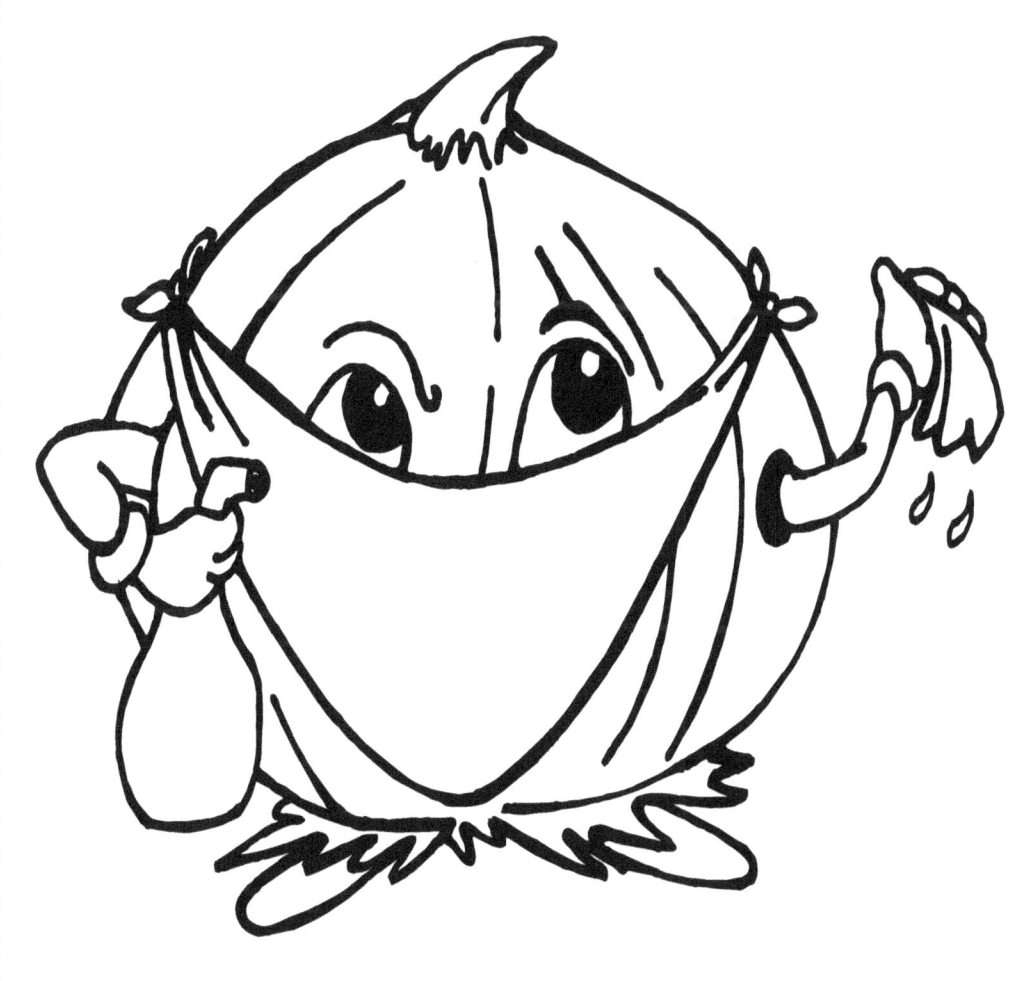

In ancient times, Pears were used to soothe the tummy ache.

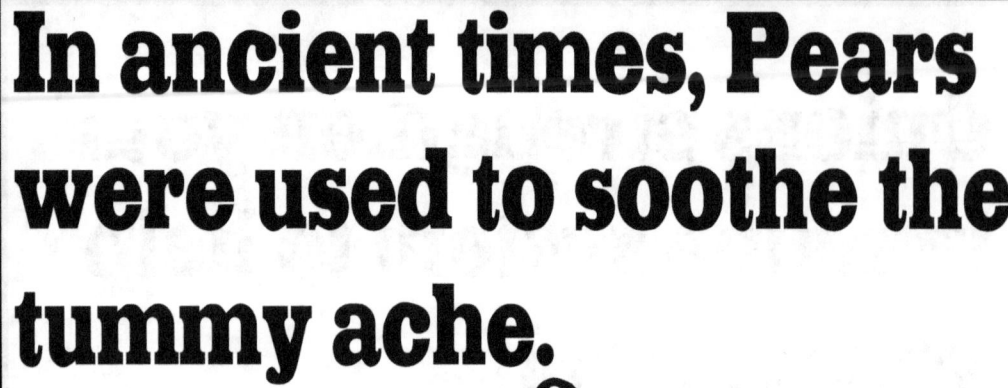

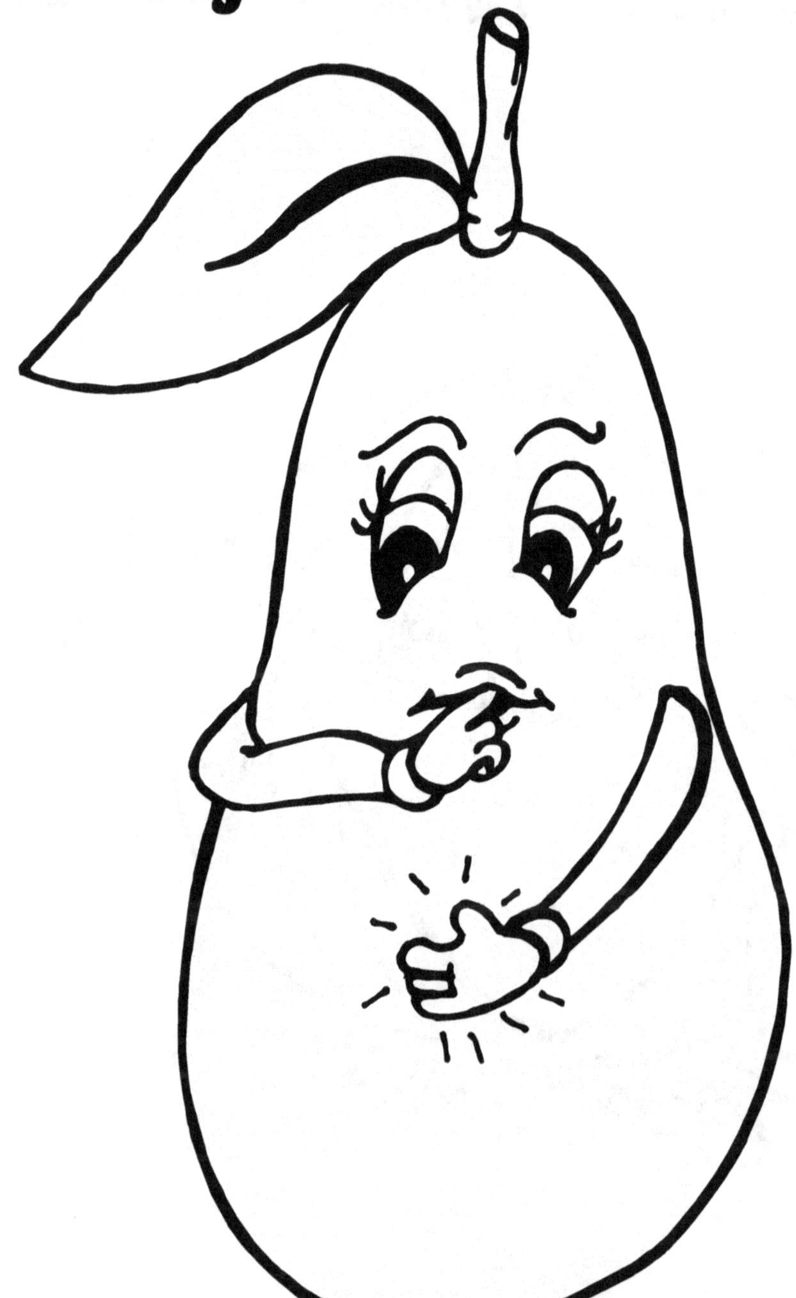

Persimmons have properties that aid in healing open cuts and wounds.

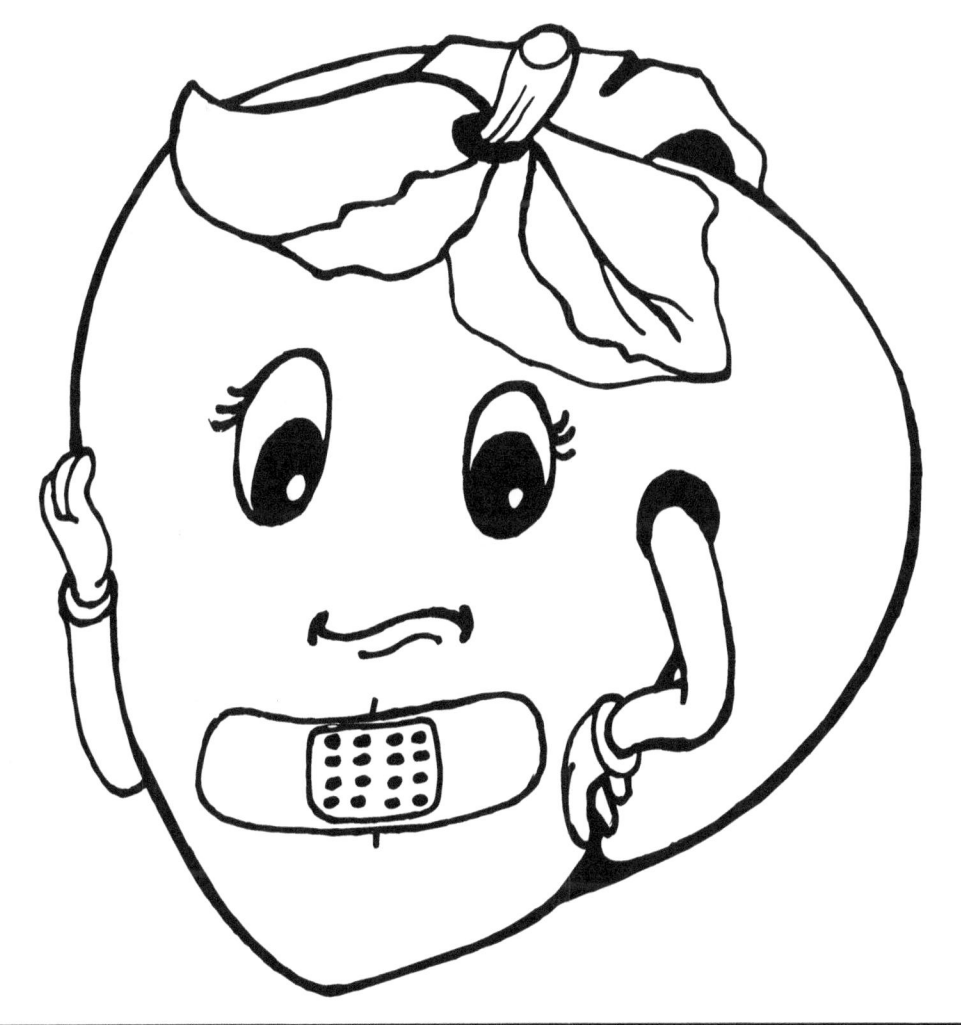

There are between 4,000 and 5,000 different species of potatoes cultivated, and 200 species of wild potatoes. The potato is the most popular vegetable world-wide. The largest potato ever grown weighed 370-lb (pounds).

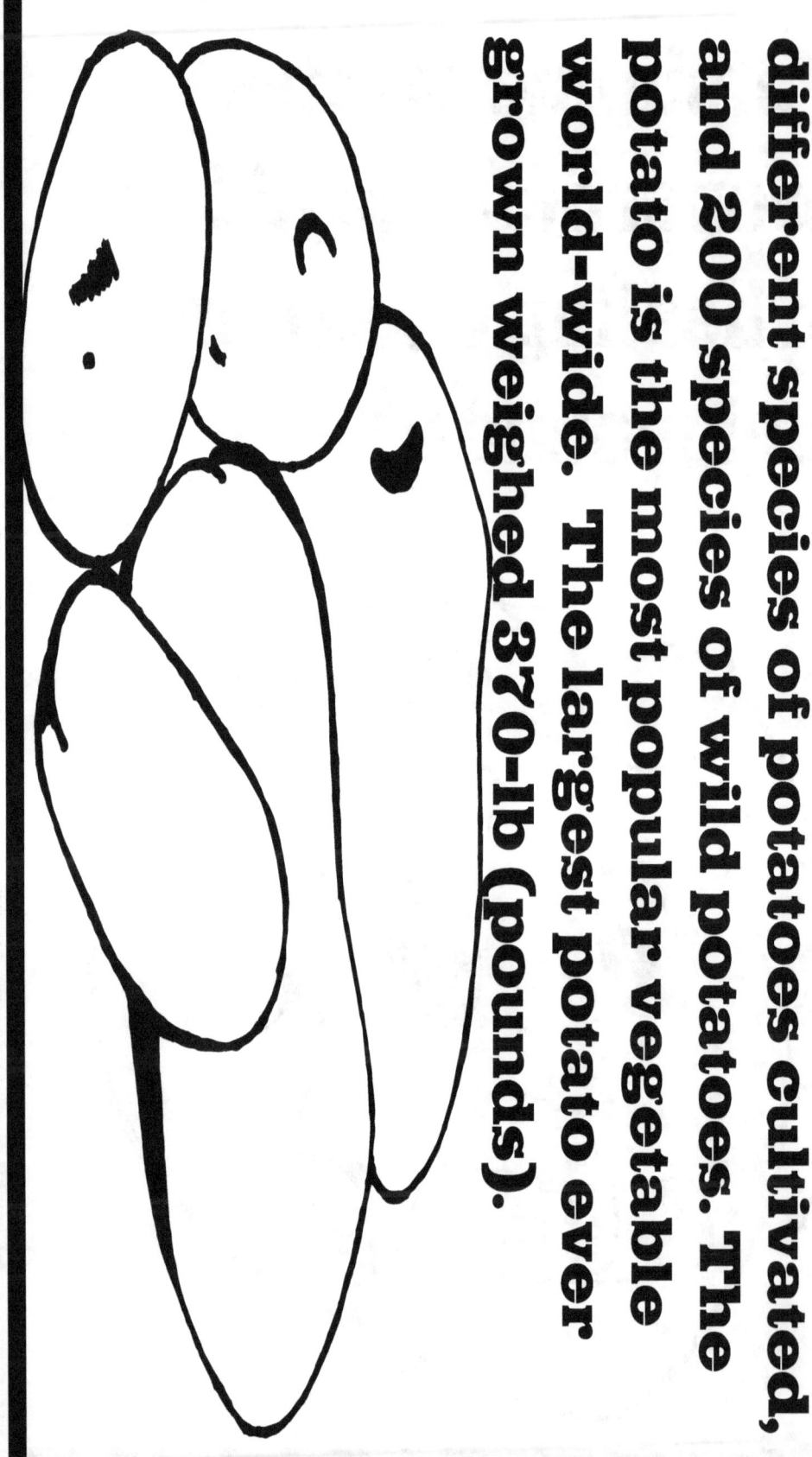

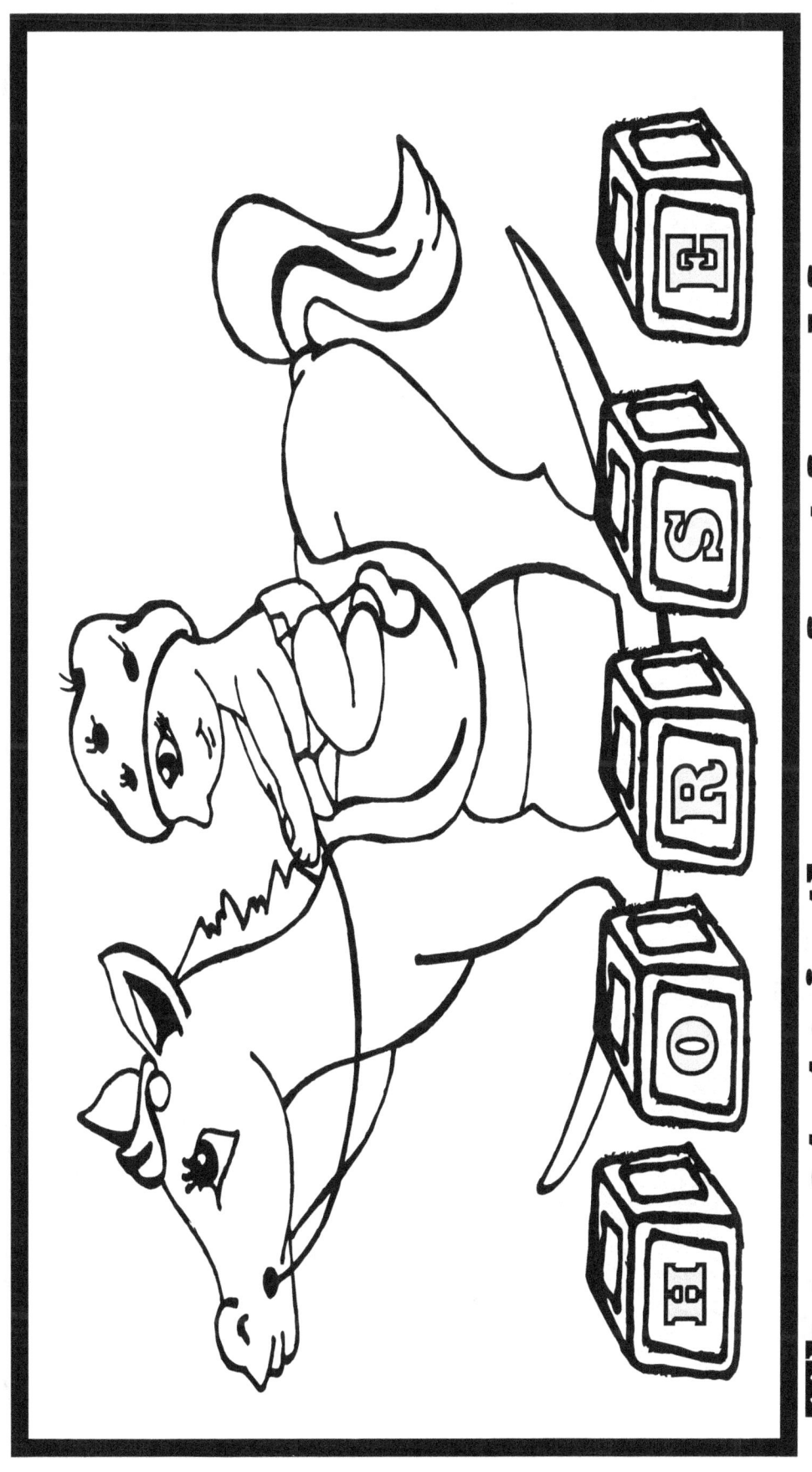

The potato is the perfect food for athletes because it contains 32% vitamin B6.

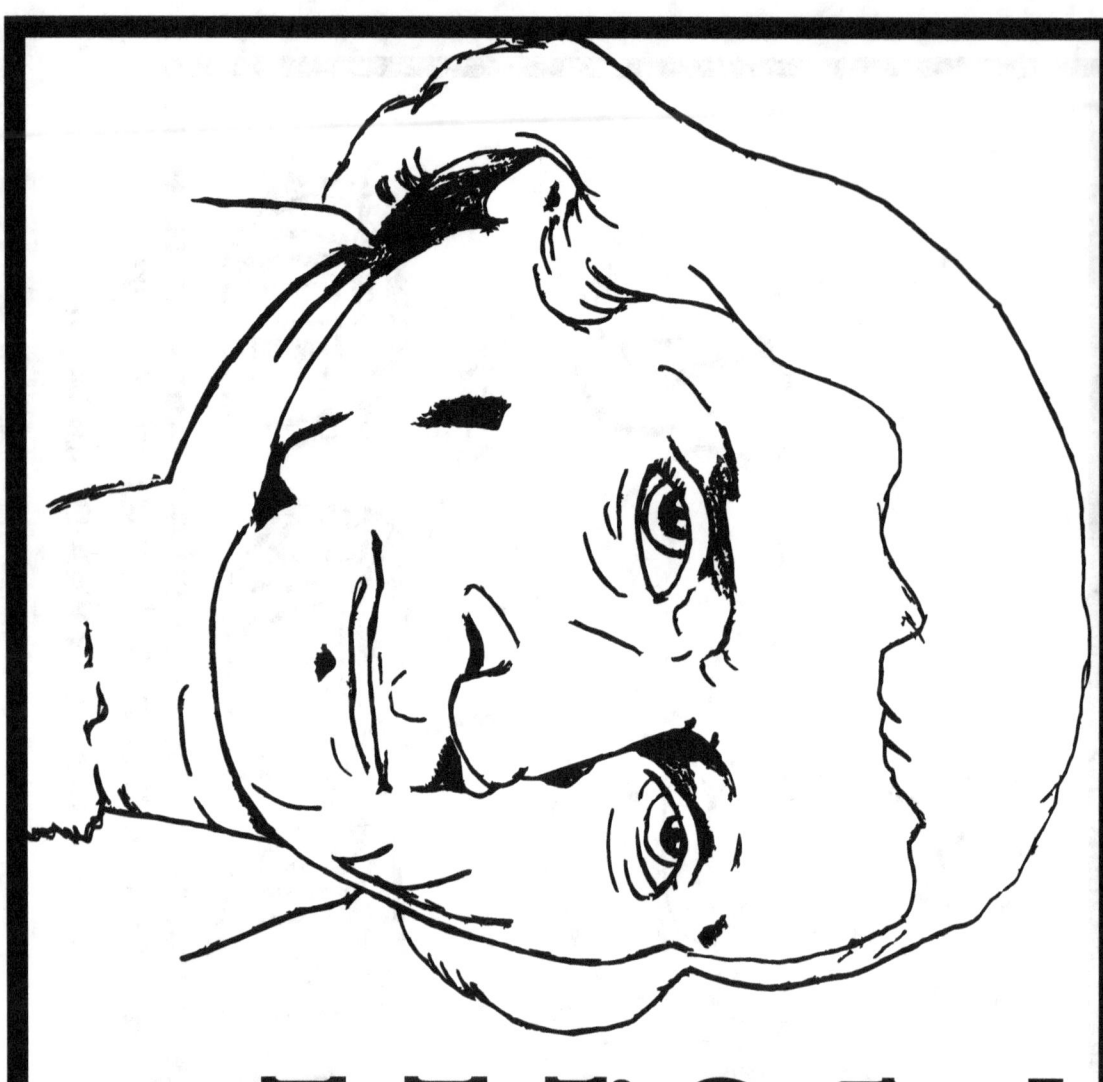

Thomas Jefferson
the 3rd President
of the United States
introduced French
Fries at a White
House dinner in
1802.

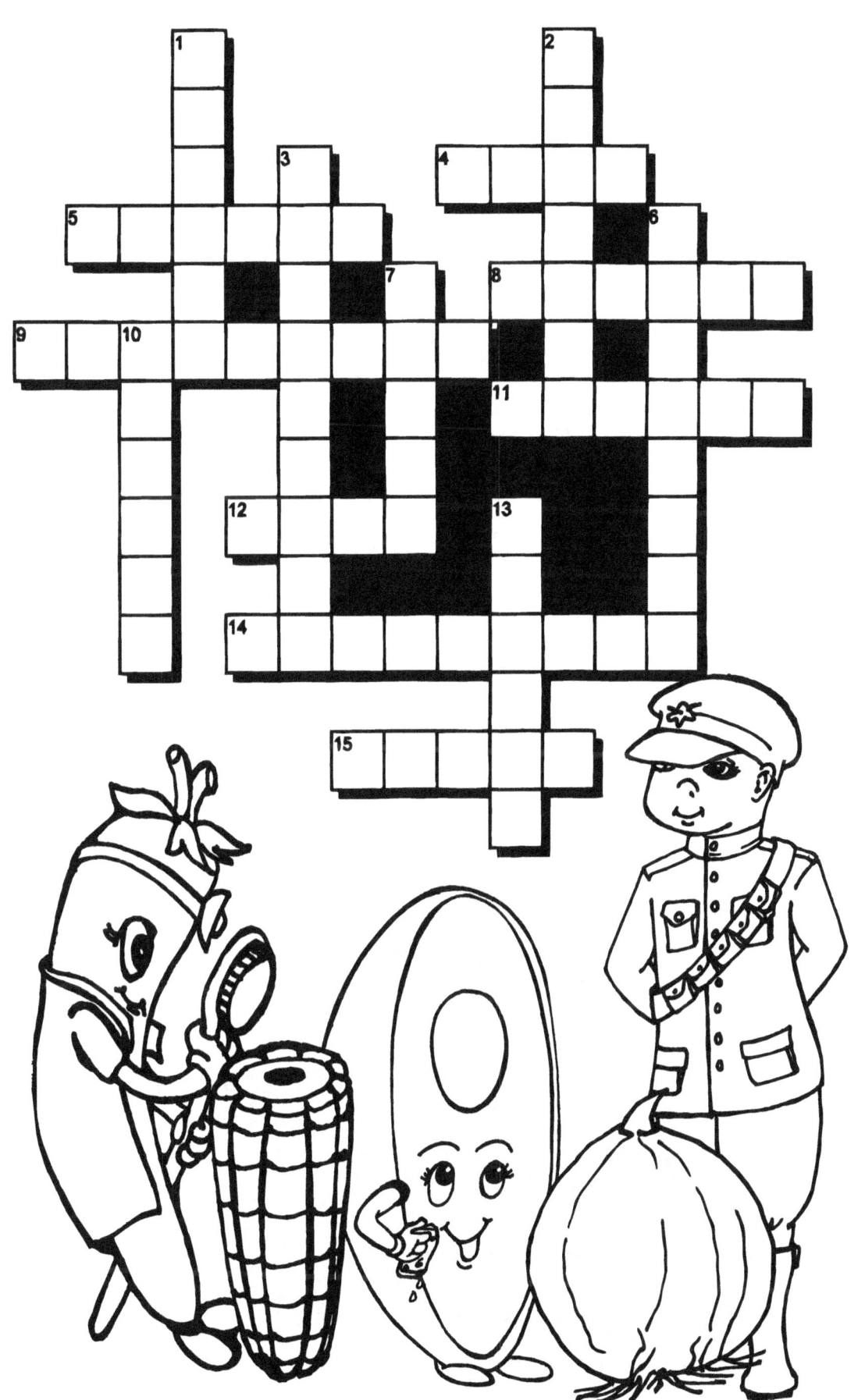

DOWN

1: I WAS USED AS AN ANTISEPTIC DURING BOTH WORLD WARS.

2: I ACT AS A SPONGE IN THE BODY.

3: I LOOK LIKE A GREEN PINE CONE

6: I'M GREEN AND KIDNEY SHAPED

7: I MAKE YOU CRY.

10: I CAN CLEAN YOUR MOUTH AFTER EATING.

13: I HELP LETTUCE MAKE A SALAD.

ACROSS

4: I'M GOOD FOR TUMMY ACHES.

5: I"M A GOOD SNACK WITH PEANUT BUTTER.

8: I HELP YOUR BRAIN FUNCTION.

9: I'M LONG, GREEN, AND FULL OF WATER, BUT I'M NOT A MELON.

11: I CAN BE MASHED, BAKED, GRILLED, AND FIRED, AND STILL TASTE GOOD.

12: I'M AN EAR WITH HUSK.

14: I HELP HEAL CUTS AND WOUNDS.

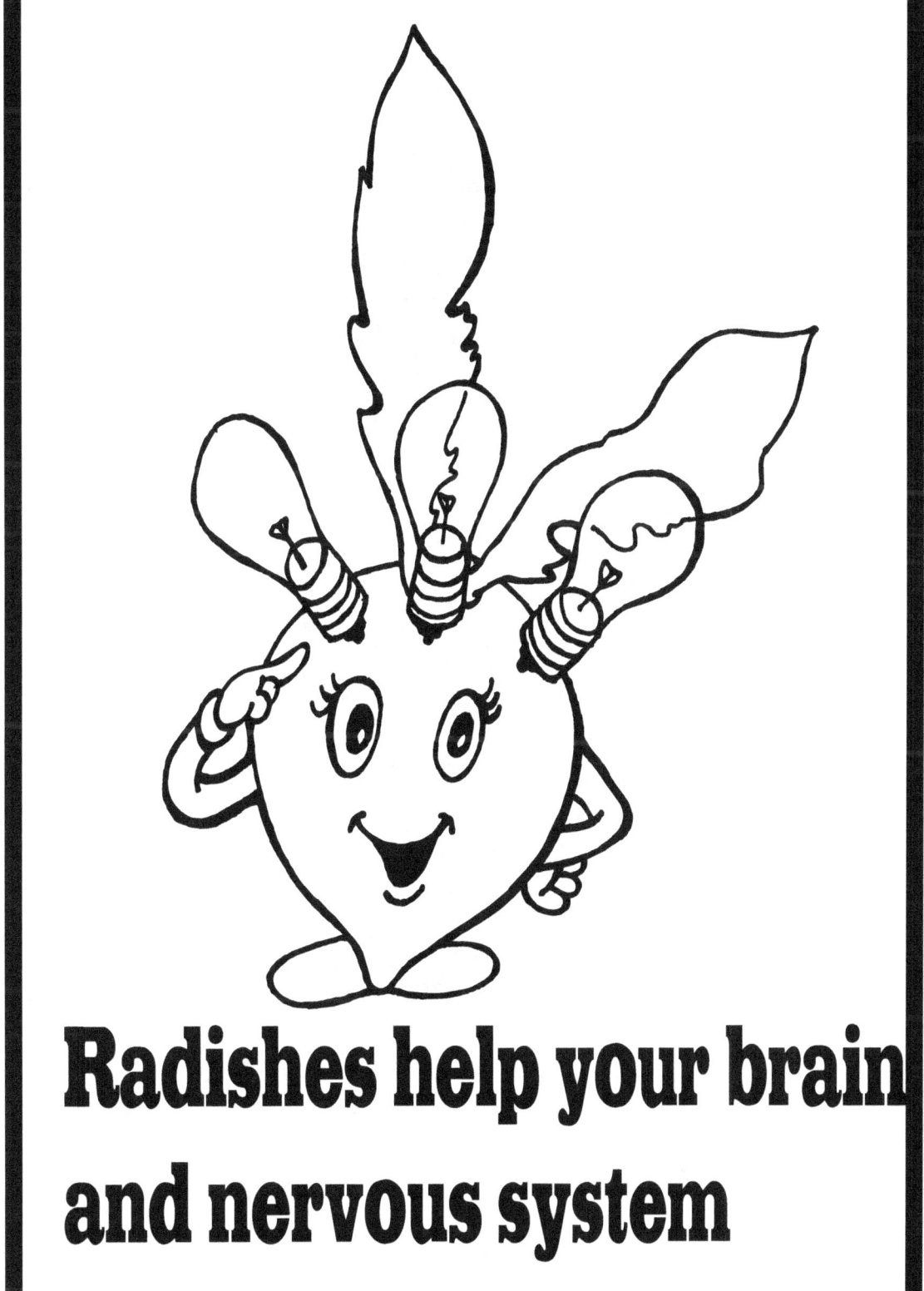

Radishes help your brain and nervous system function normally.

Rutabaga is good for the heart, helps build muscles, and aids in digesting food.

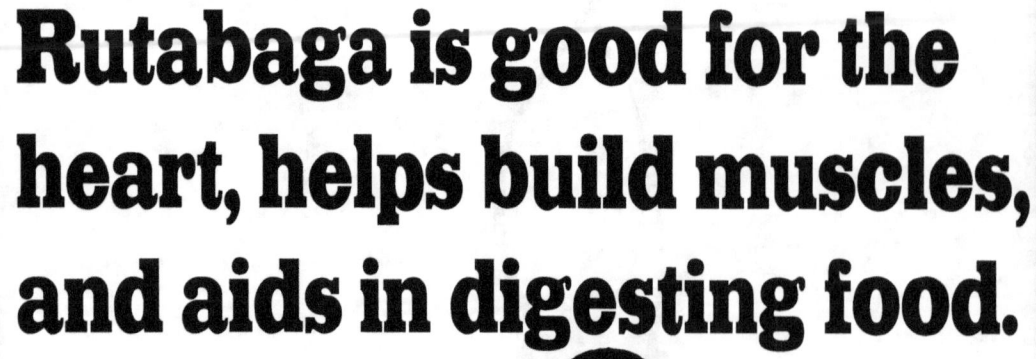

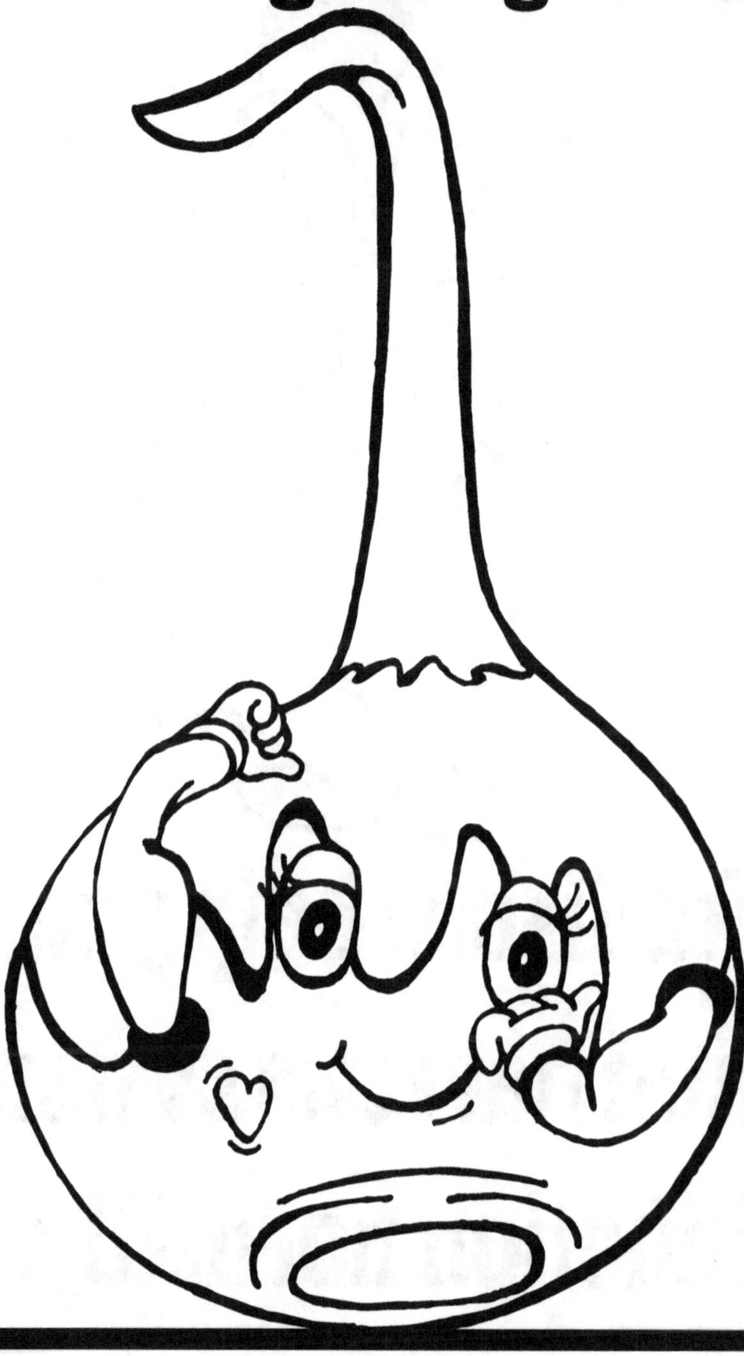

Cut the pieces out and put Baby Spud back together right.

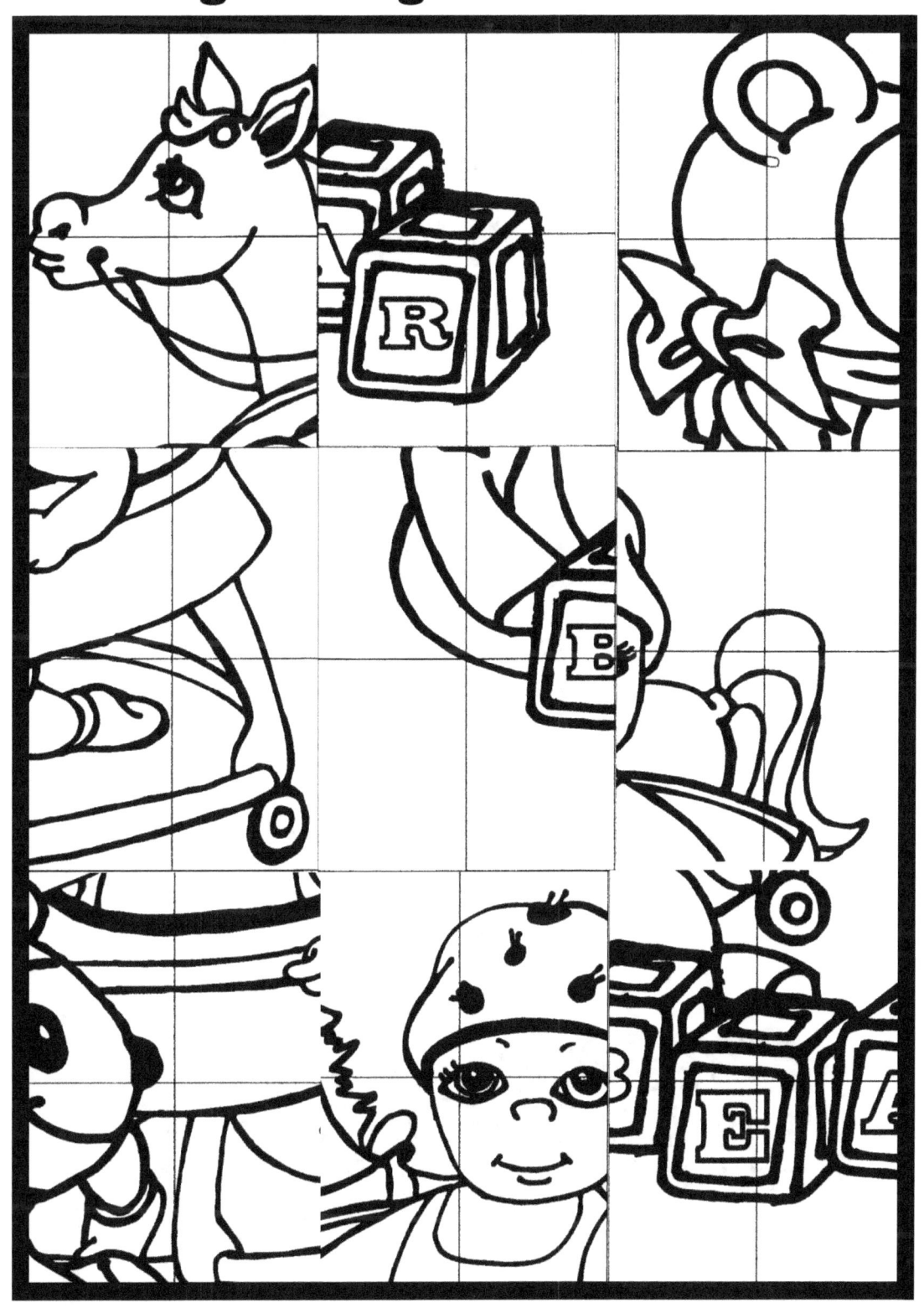

Only the root, can be eaten. The leaves, stems, and all other portions of the potato contain Glycoalkaloid and are poisonous. Wild potatoes have an extremely high content of Glycoalkaloid.

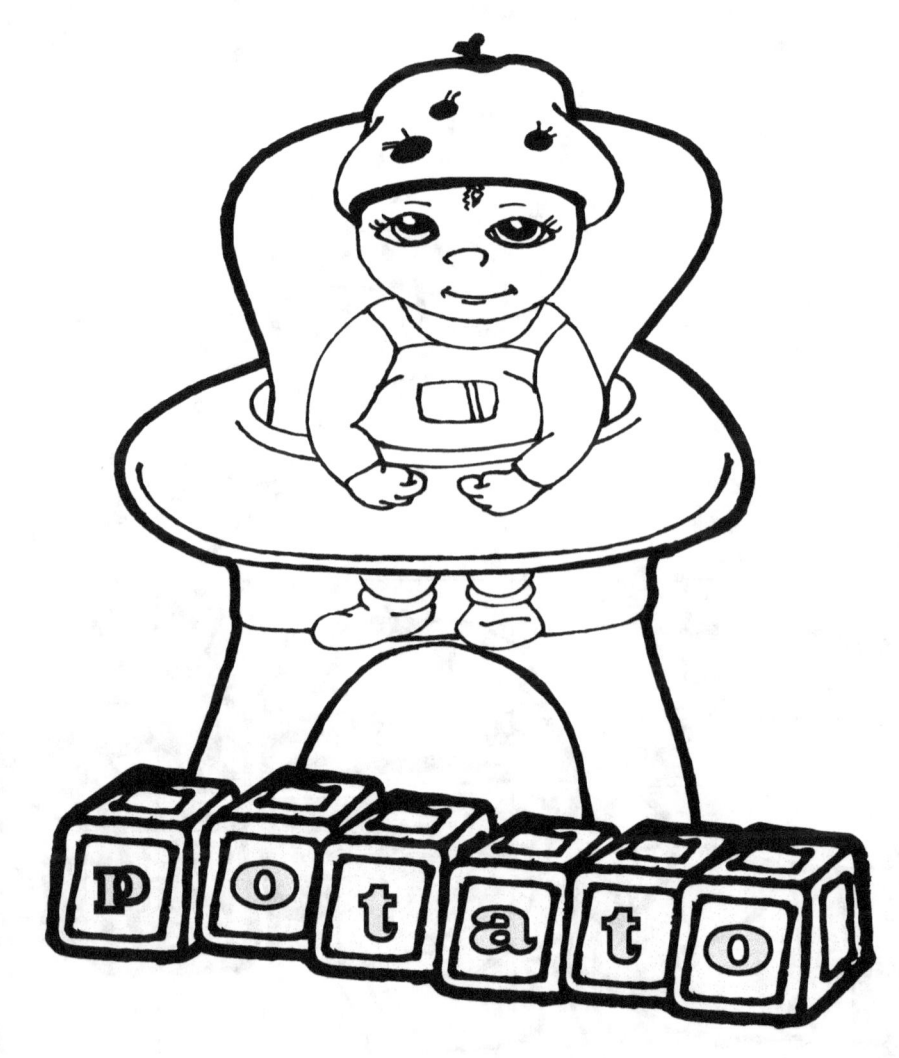

If you had 11 strawberries and you took 11 stawberries away, what would you have?

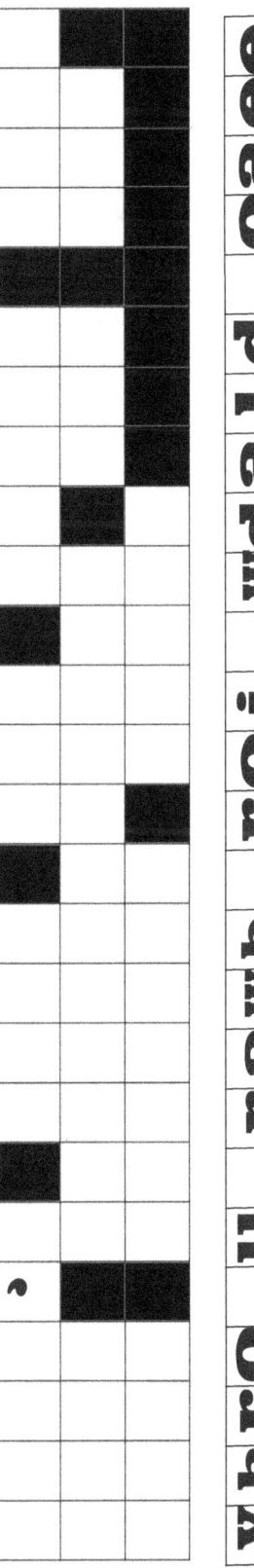

vhro	u	rawb	roi	wdald	oaee
teay	t	eas	peyrhis	und	hnv
zert	snhap	yy	cuelo

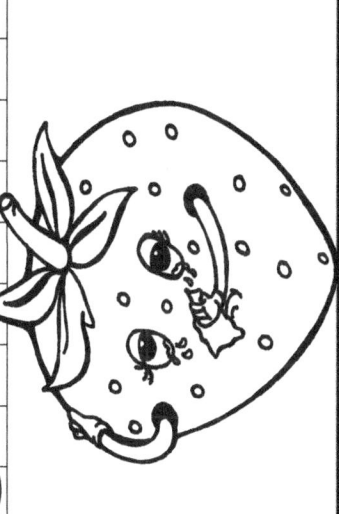

Using the letter in the second graph, fill in the blanks in the first graph to reveal the punch line to this joke.

Due to some mushrooms being poinous, people

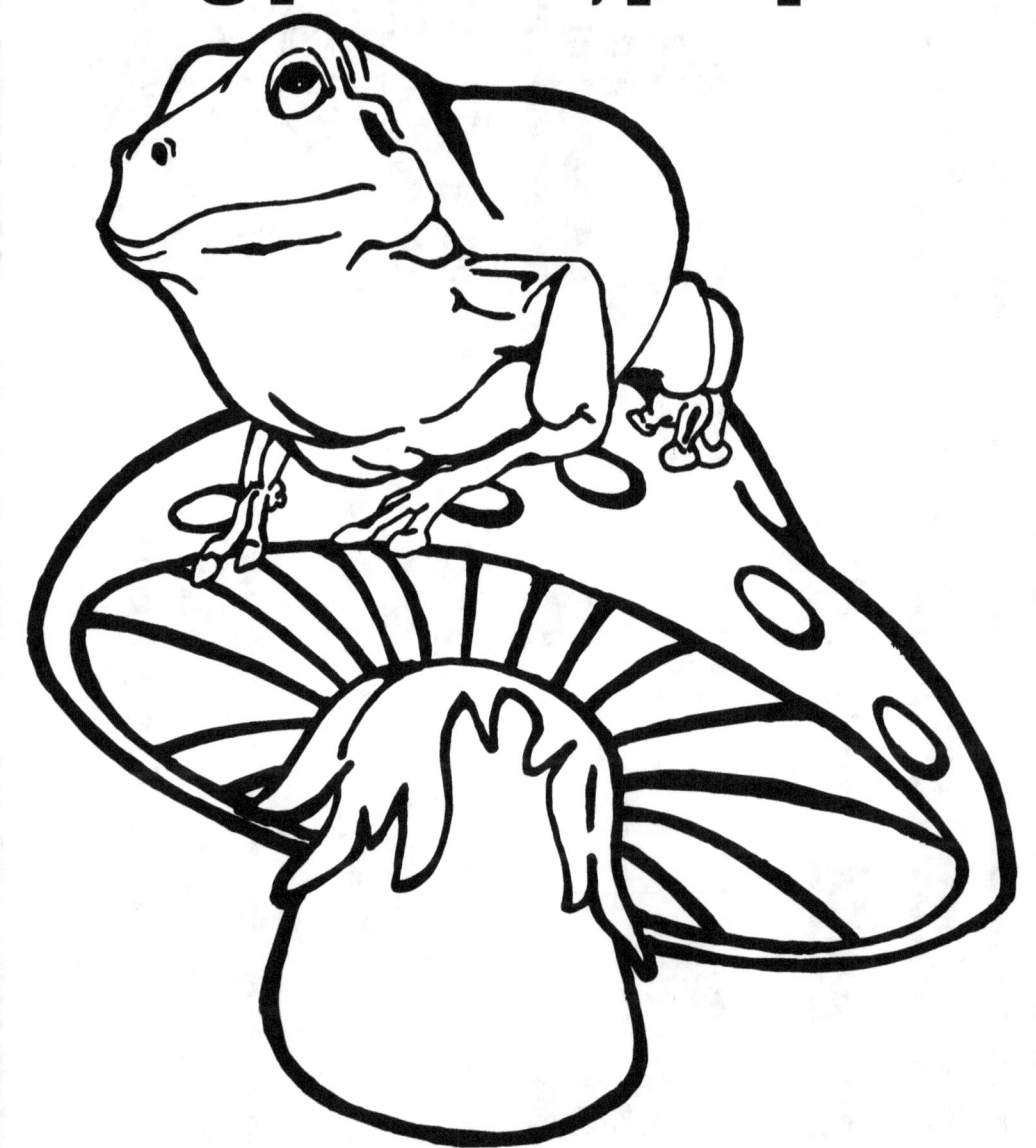

began calling them TOADSTOOLS

Although the tomato originated in the South American Andes, they were first consumed in Mexico. The name tomato comes from "tomatotl" the Nahautl word for the fruit.

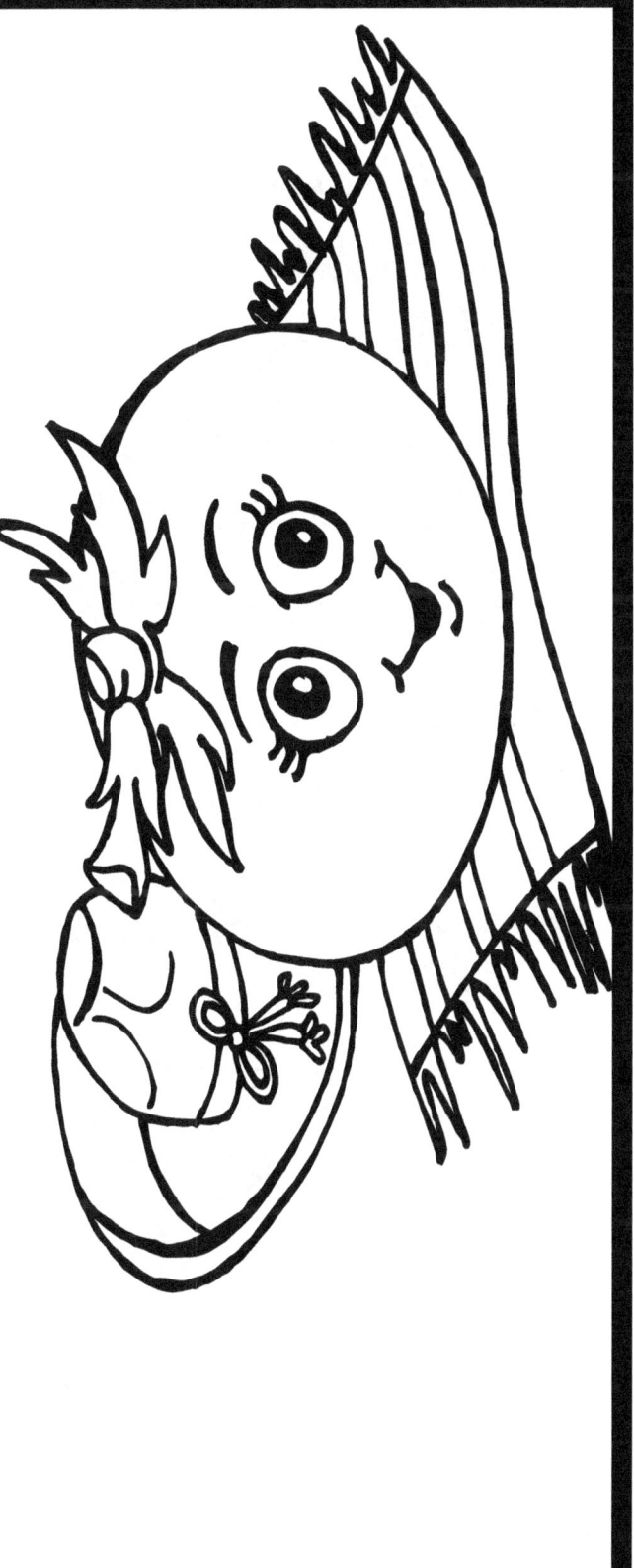

In many countries around the world, tomatoes were not eaten until the late 1500s, due to their genus.

The tomato is a member of the Nightshade Family, which includes:

Potatoes

Peppers

Eggplant

Tomatillos

Berries

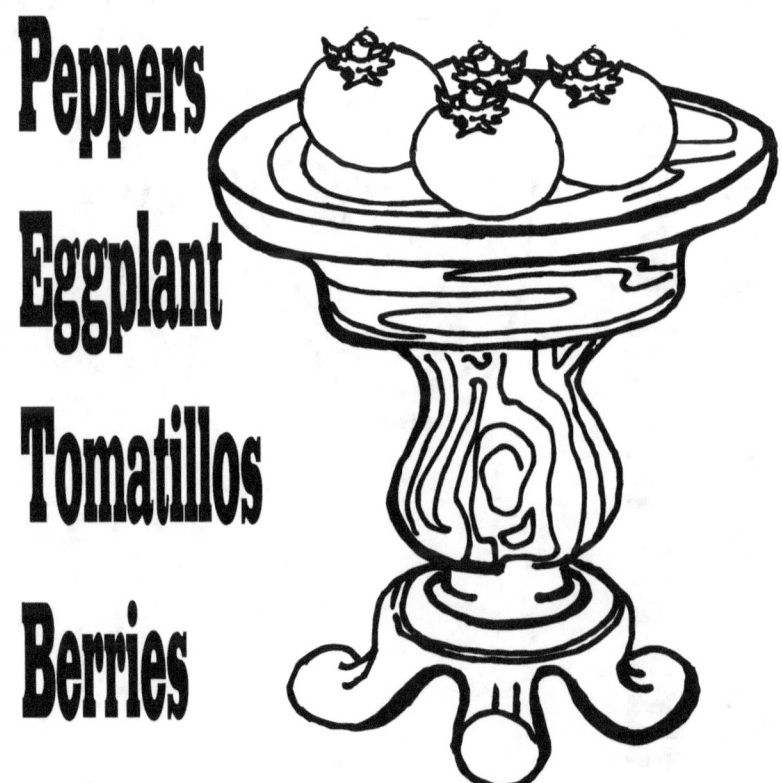

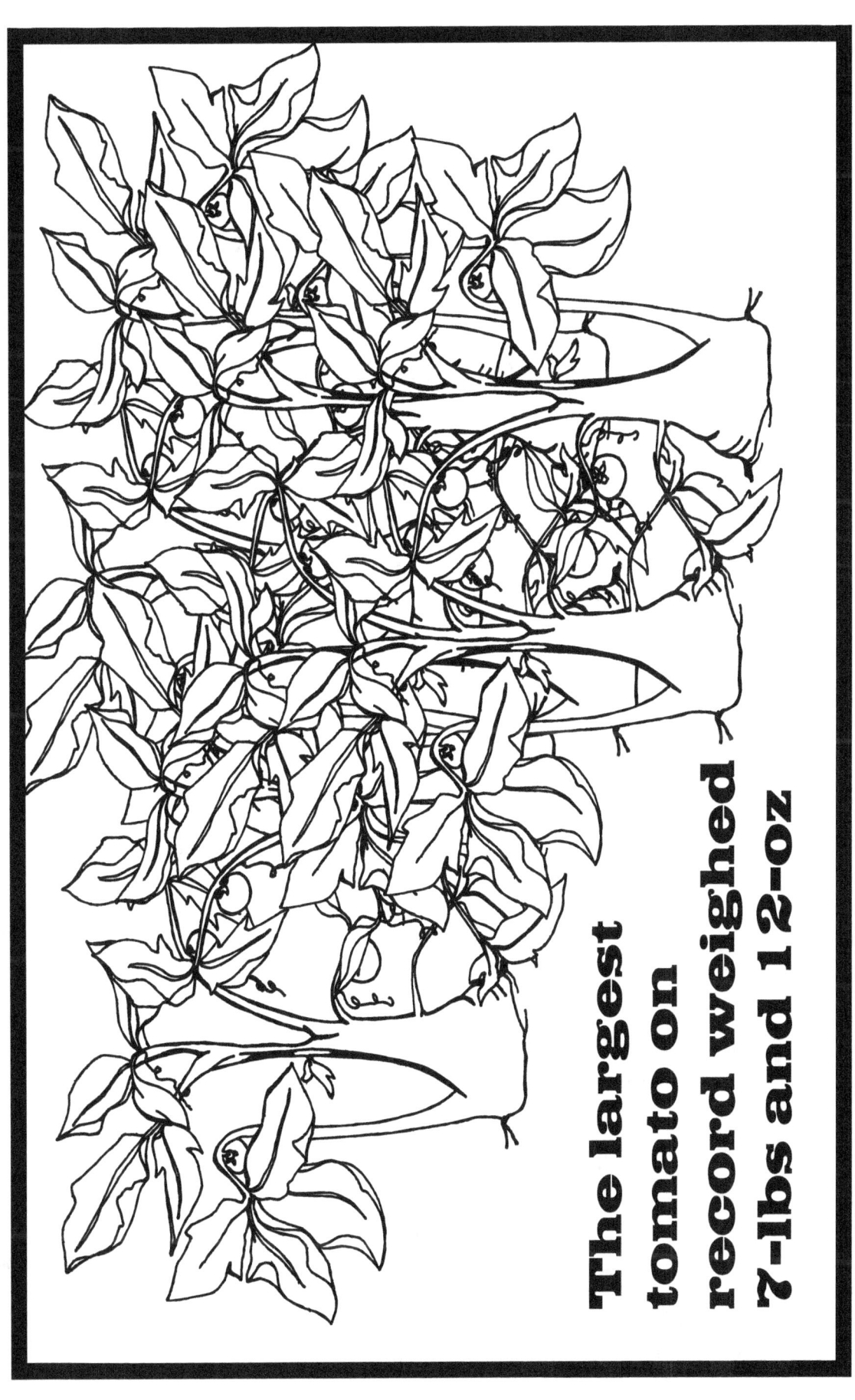

The largest
tomato on
record weighed
7-lbs and 12-oz

Weighing 1151-lbs and producing 32-thousand tomatoes, Disney"s World Resort had the largest recorded tomato plant. It lived 13 months before having to be removed due to disease.

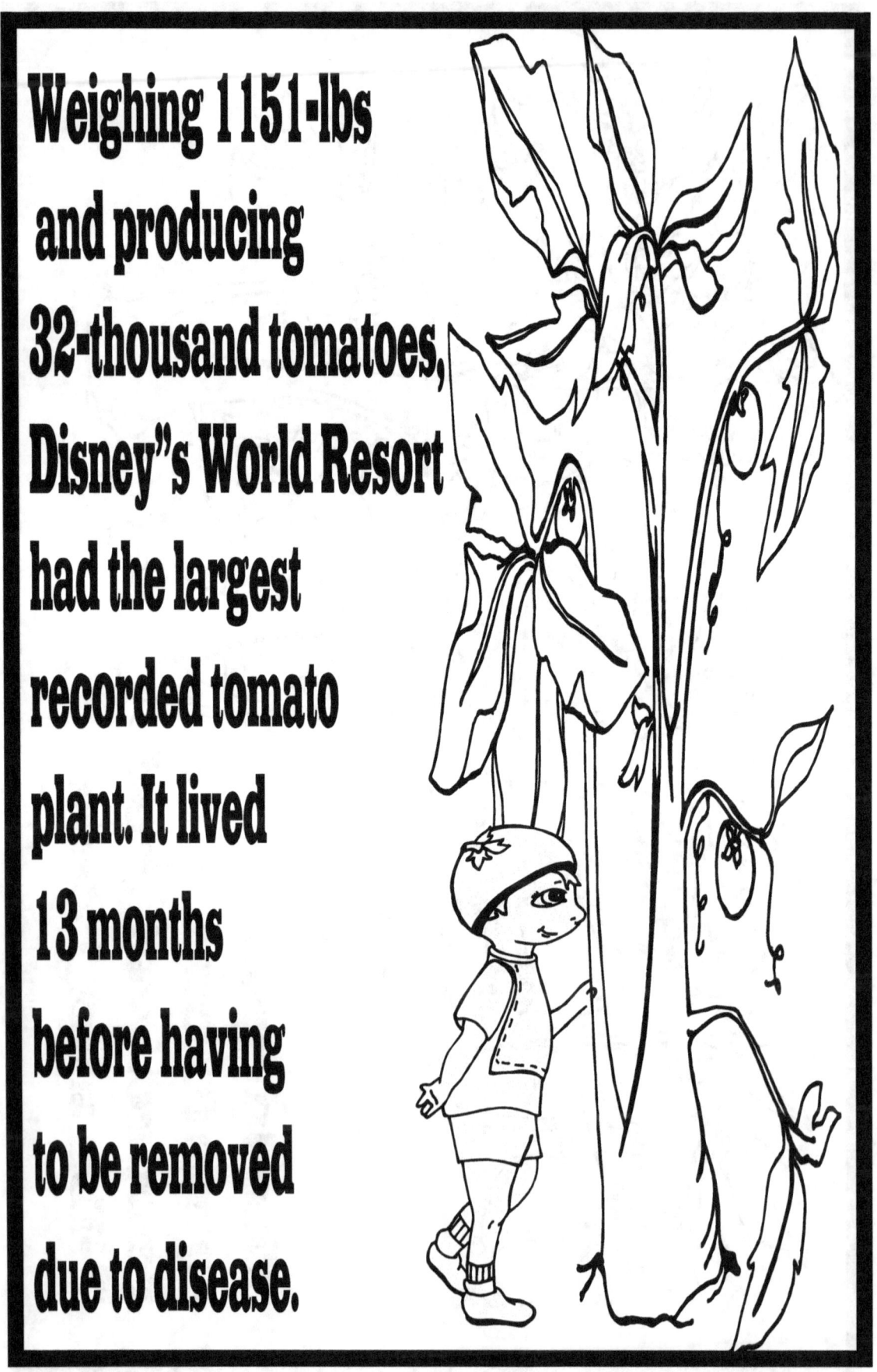

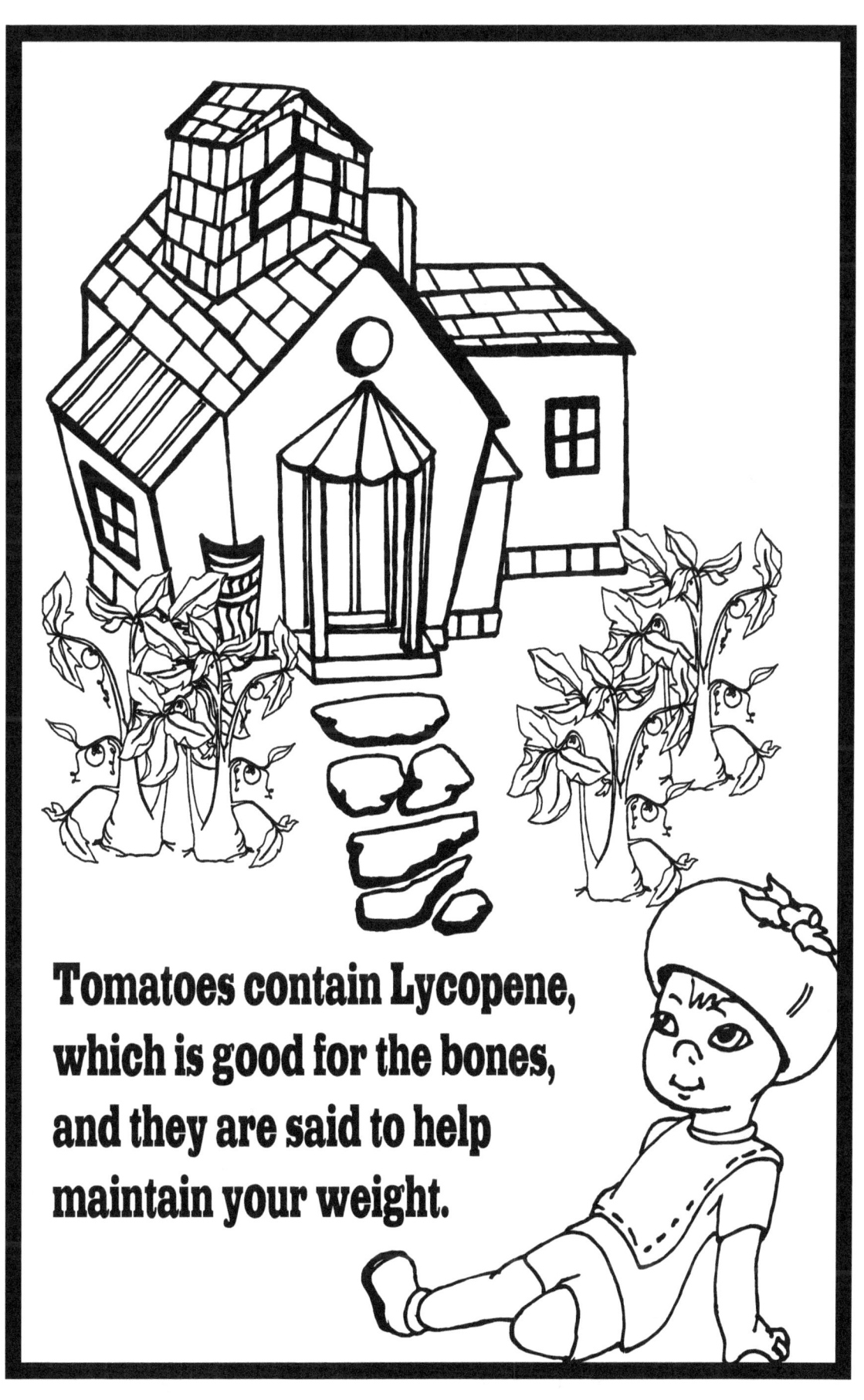

Tomatoes contain Lycopene, which is good for the bones, and they are said to help maintain your weight.

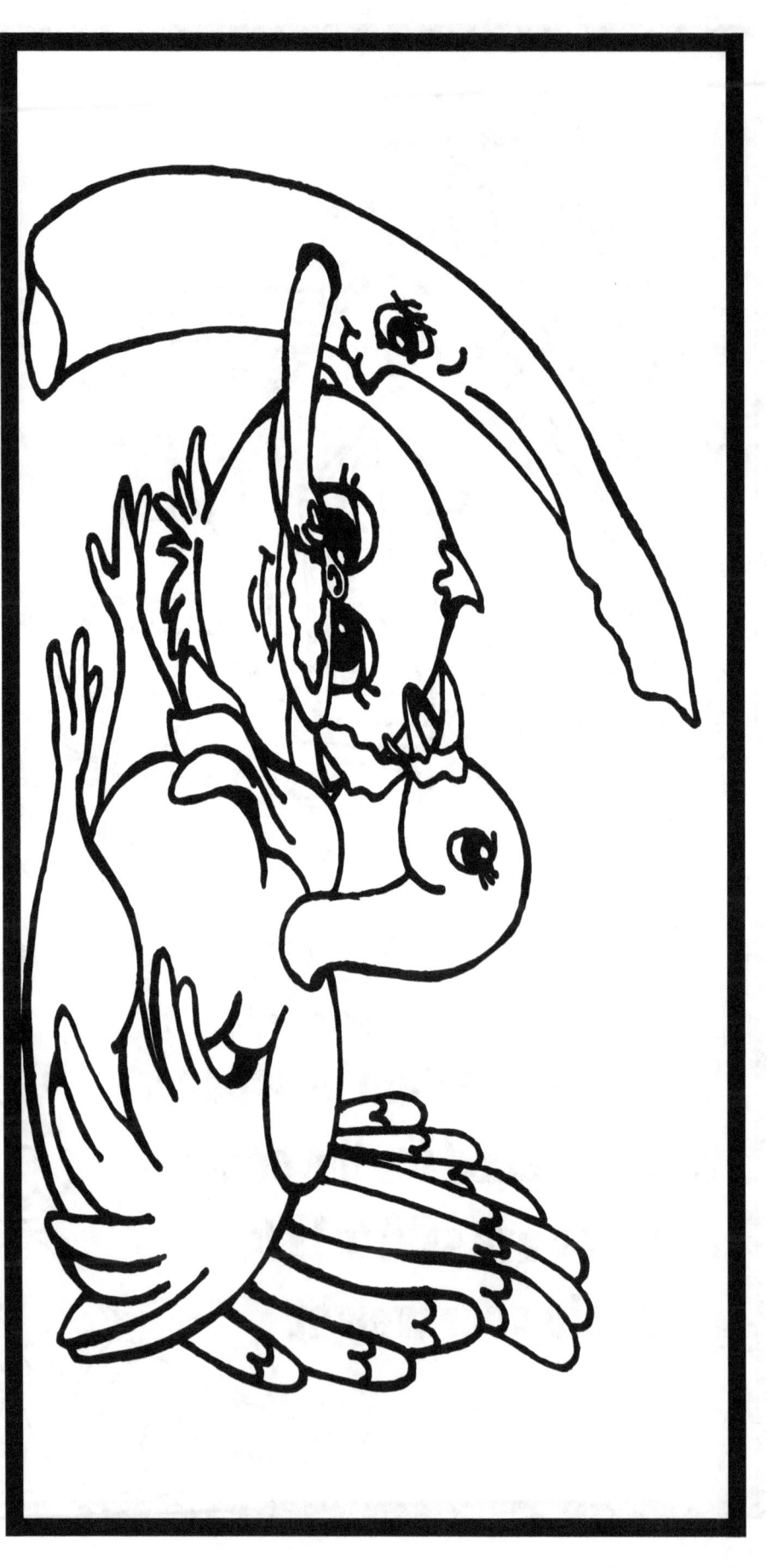

Celery and onions are two of the main ingredients in Turkey stuffing

VEGETABLE CRYPTOGRAM

2T 10

9 18 26

13 5 14

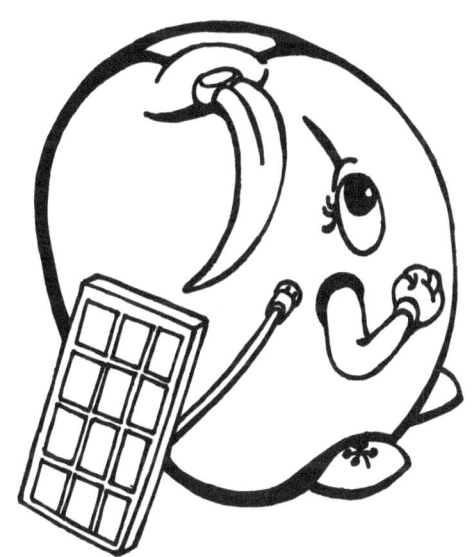

25 13 6 6 2T 13 7

9 18 26

23 2T 16 16

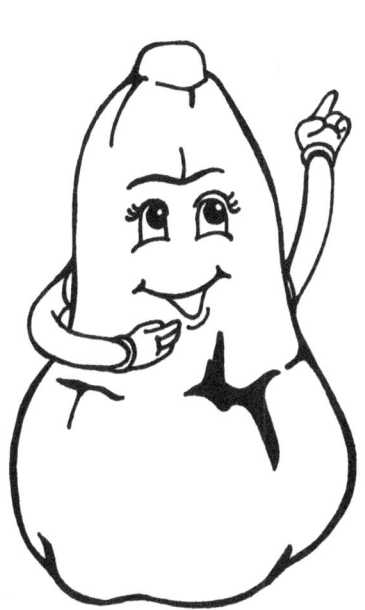

22 13

15 13 5 14 15 2T 13 4

Bushmen of the Kalahari Desert quench their thirst and make a meal of watermelon while traveling the dry arid regions. The watermelons high water content and low sugar makes it the perfect meal for weary dehydrated travelers.

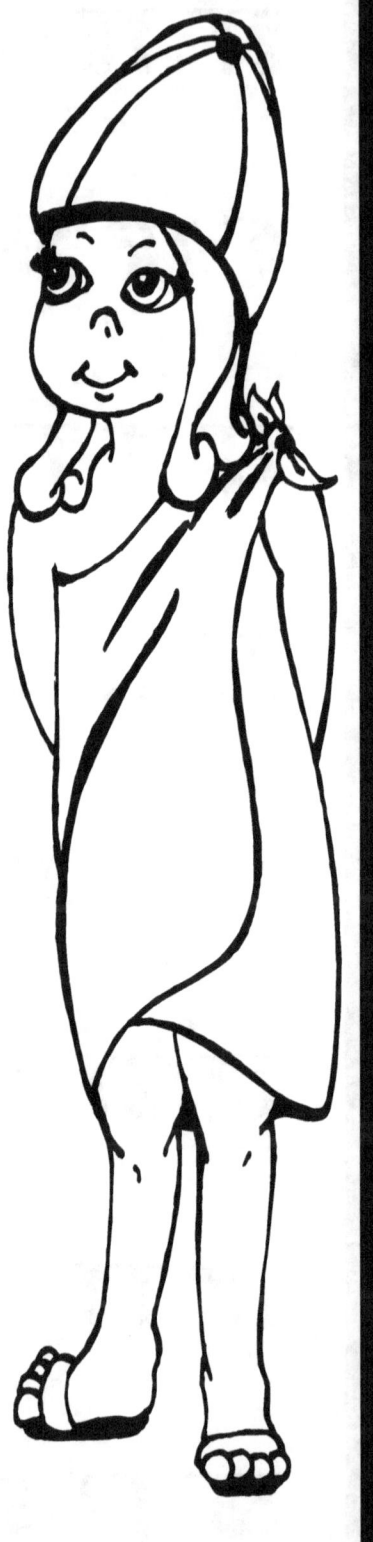

In Egypt, watermelon has been cultivated since 2000 BC.

The world's largest producer of watermelon today is China.

44 of the 50 United States are able to grow watermelon

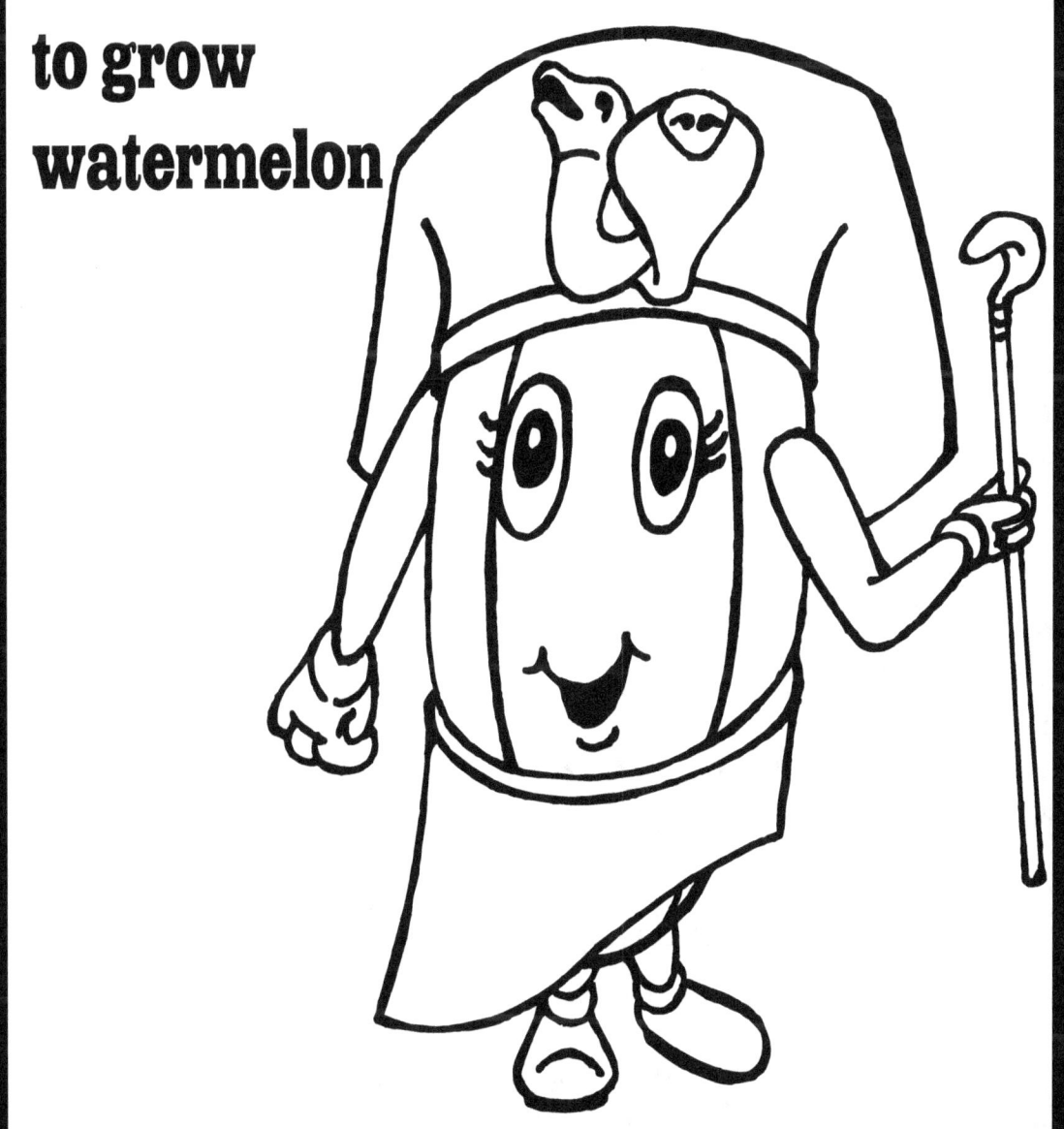

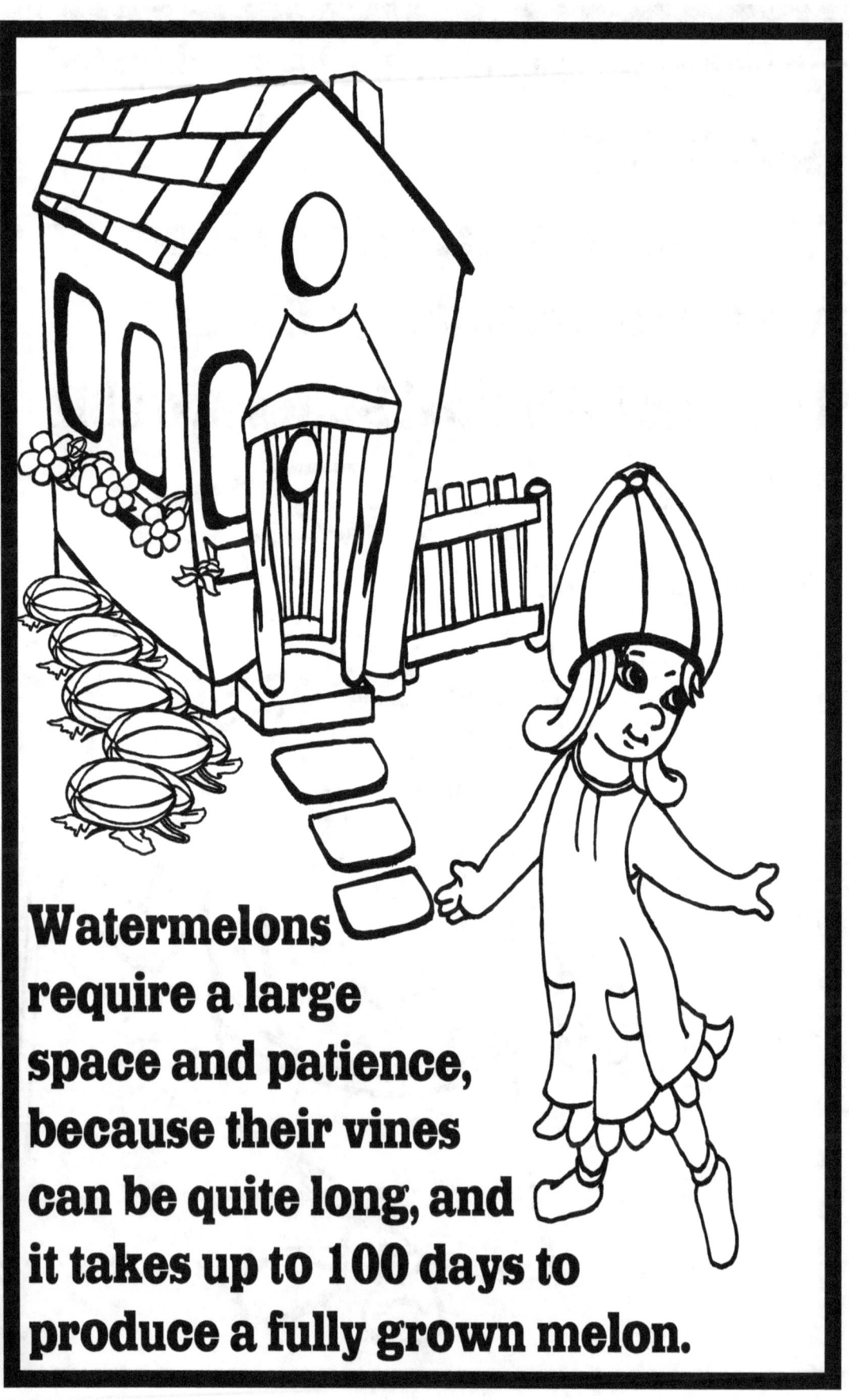

Watermelons require a large space and patience, because their vines can be quite long, and it takes up to 100 days to produce a fully grown melon.

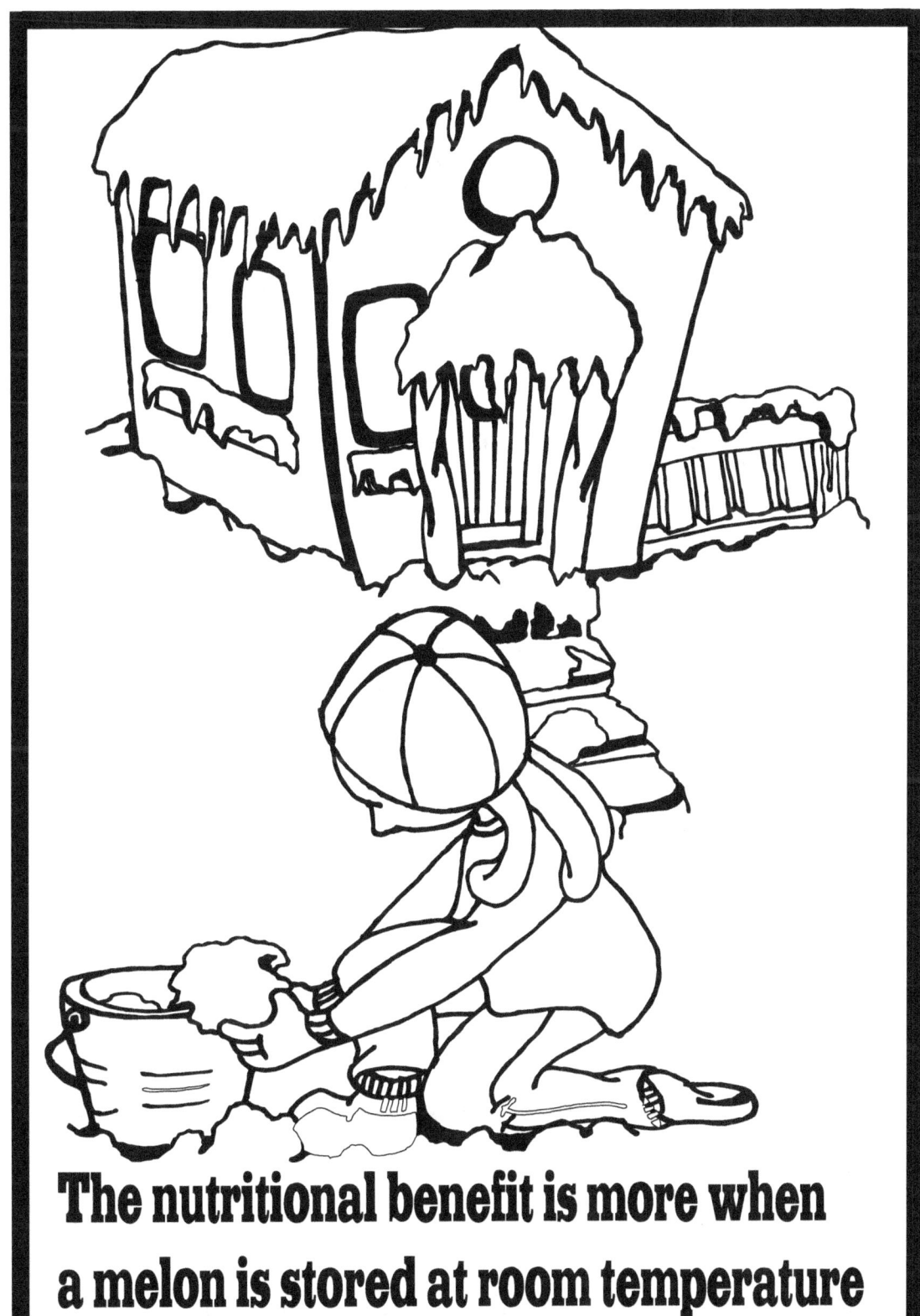

The nutritional benefit is more when a melon is stored at room temperature rather than in the refrigerator.

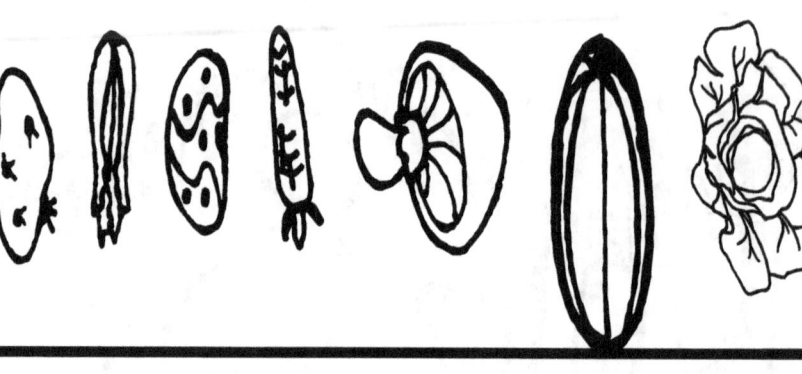

Who Am I?

1: I'm red and delicious

2: I'm the greenest green you've ever seen

3: I have freckles

4: I'm good when steamed

5: I'm orange all over

6: I'm a stalk

7: I'm great with onions

8: Use me to make salad

9: They call me toadstool

10: I make big potatoes

11: I can make paste

12: I'm green outside and red inside

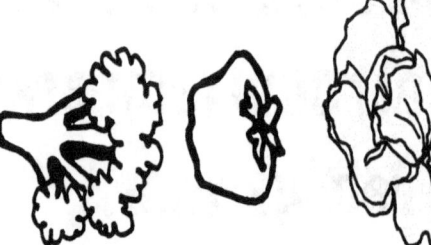
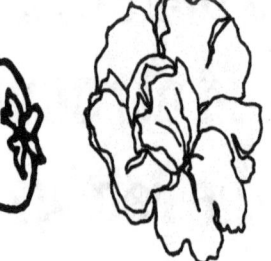
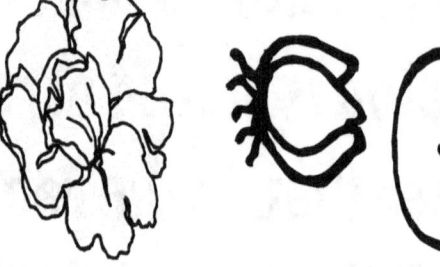
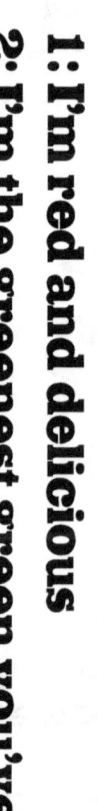

Draw a line to the vegetable or fruit that matches the desciption.

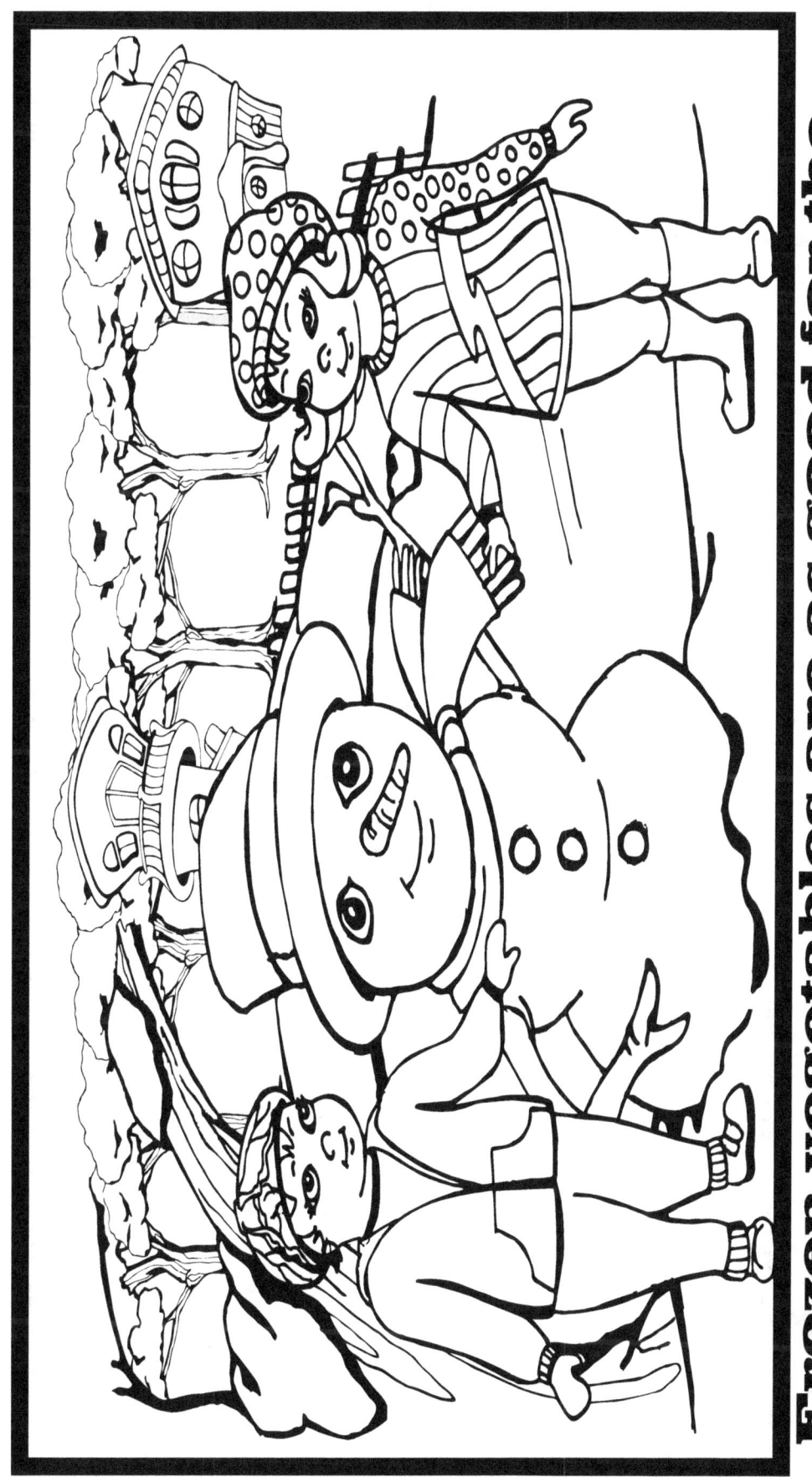

Frozen vegetables are as good for the body as fresh because they are picked fresh and immediately frozen.

Although lettuce is a very healthy vegetable, it cannot be frozen, canned, or pickled.

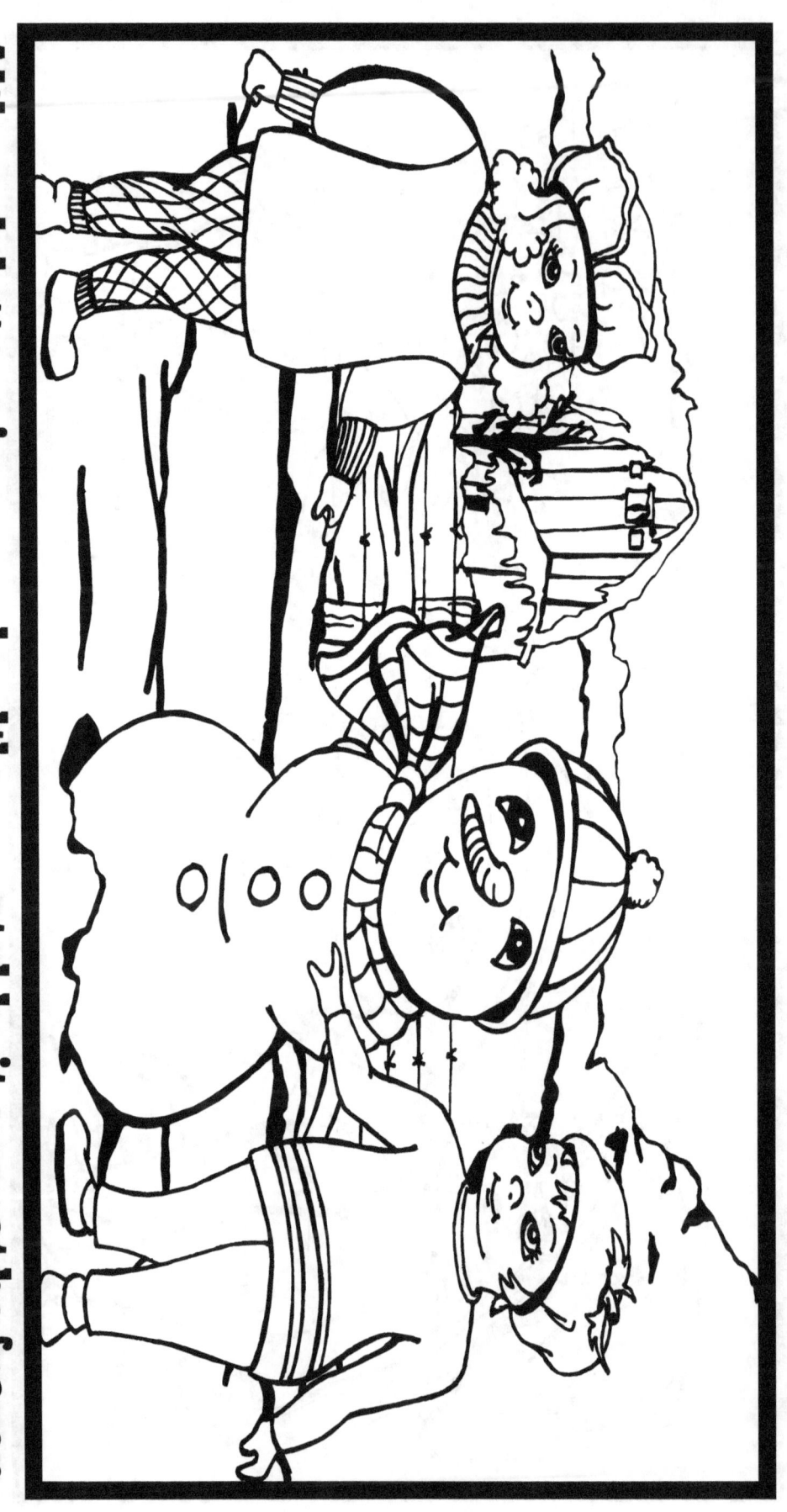

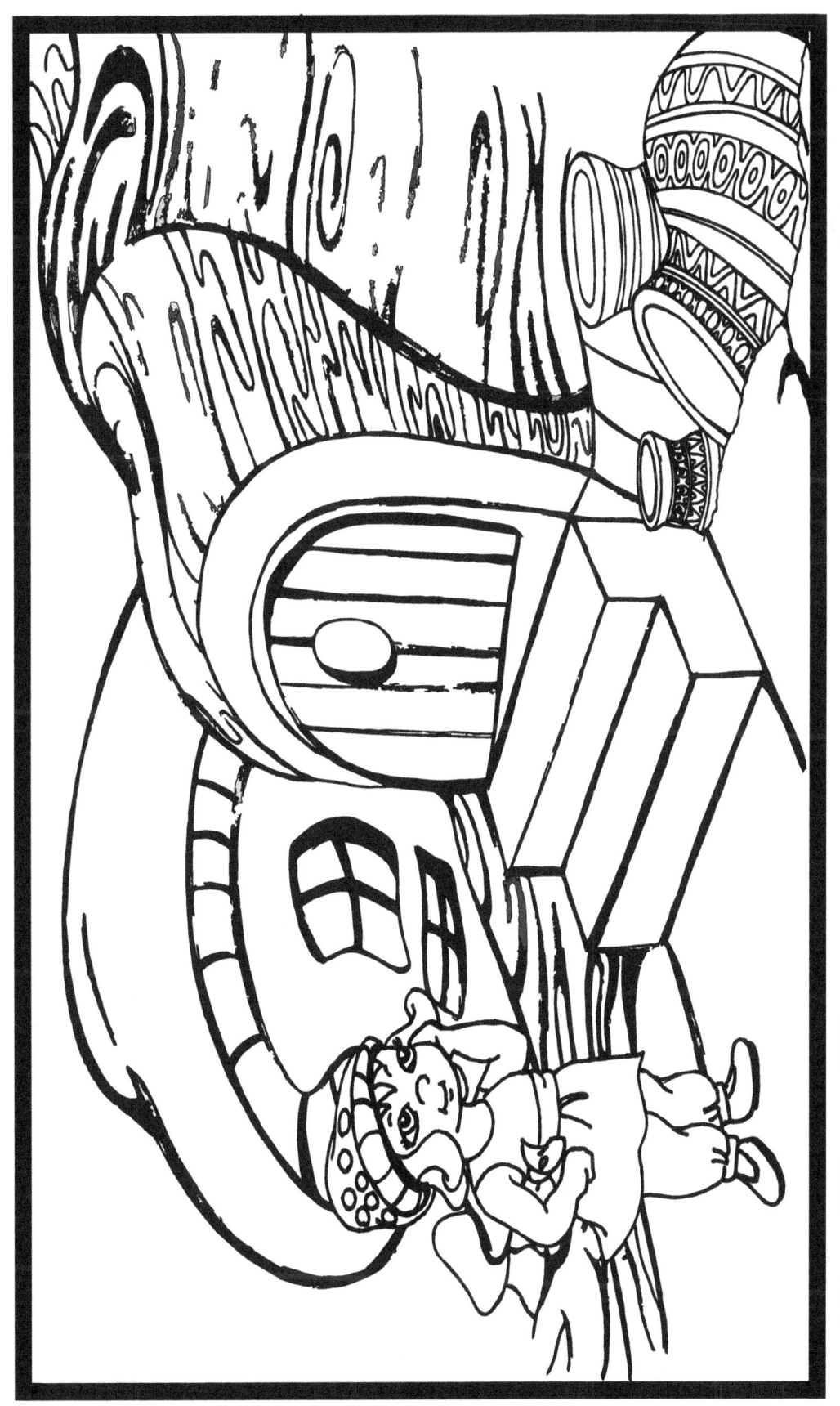

Truffles, like other mushrooms, are a fungus and are found near the base of certian trees

FIVE AND FIVE MAKE

TEN, BUT FIVE AND

A MOM AND DAD

MAKE A HAPPY FAMILY

VIFE NAD VIFE EKMA

_____ _____ _____ _____

ENT, UBT VIFE NAD

_____ _____ _____ _____

A OMM NAD DDA

_____ _____ _____

EKMA A PAHPY IMYLFA

_____ _____ _____ _____

Unscramble the words to see
the message.

The key to the Cryptograms:

1: J	14: T
2: N	15: H
3: C	16: L
4: R	17: X
5: A	18: O
6: G	19: D
7: S	20: P
8: Z	21: I
9: Y	22: B
10: F	23: W
11: Q	24: M
12: K	25: V
13: E	26: U

Answers to Crossword Puzzle:

Down

1: Garlic
2: Avacado
3: Artichoke
6: Limabean
7: Onion
10: Carrot
13: Tomato

Across

4: Pear
5: Celery
8: Radish
9: Zucchinni
11: Potato
12: Corn
14: Persimmon
15: Beets

Hint: One of the fruits is misspelled.
Did you figure out which one it is?

If you had 11 strawberries and you took 11 stawberries away, what would you have?

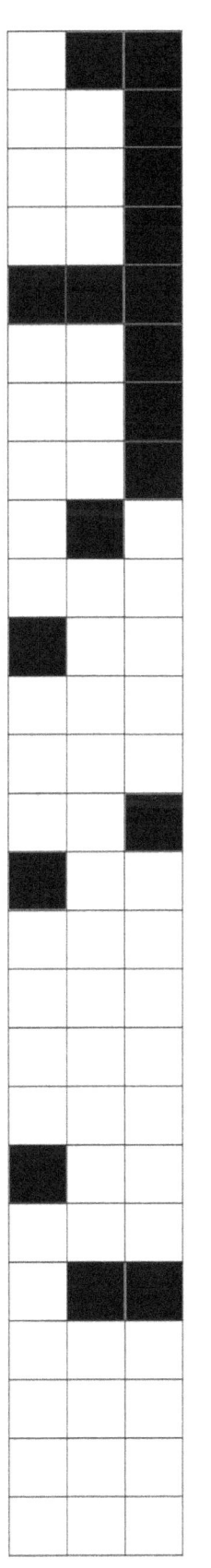

That's easy. You would have zero strawberries and one very unhappy child.

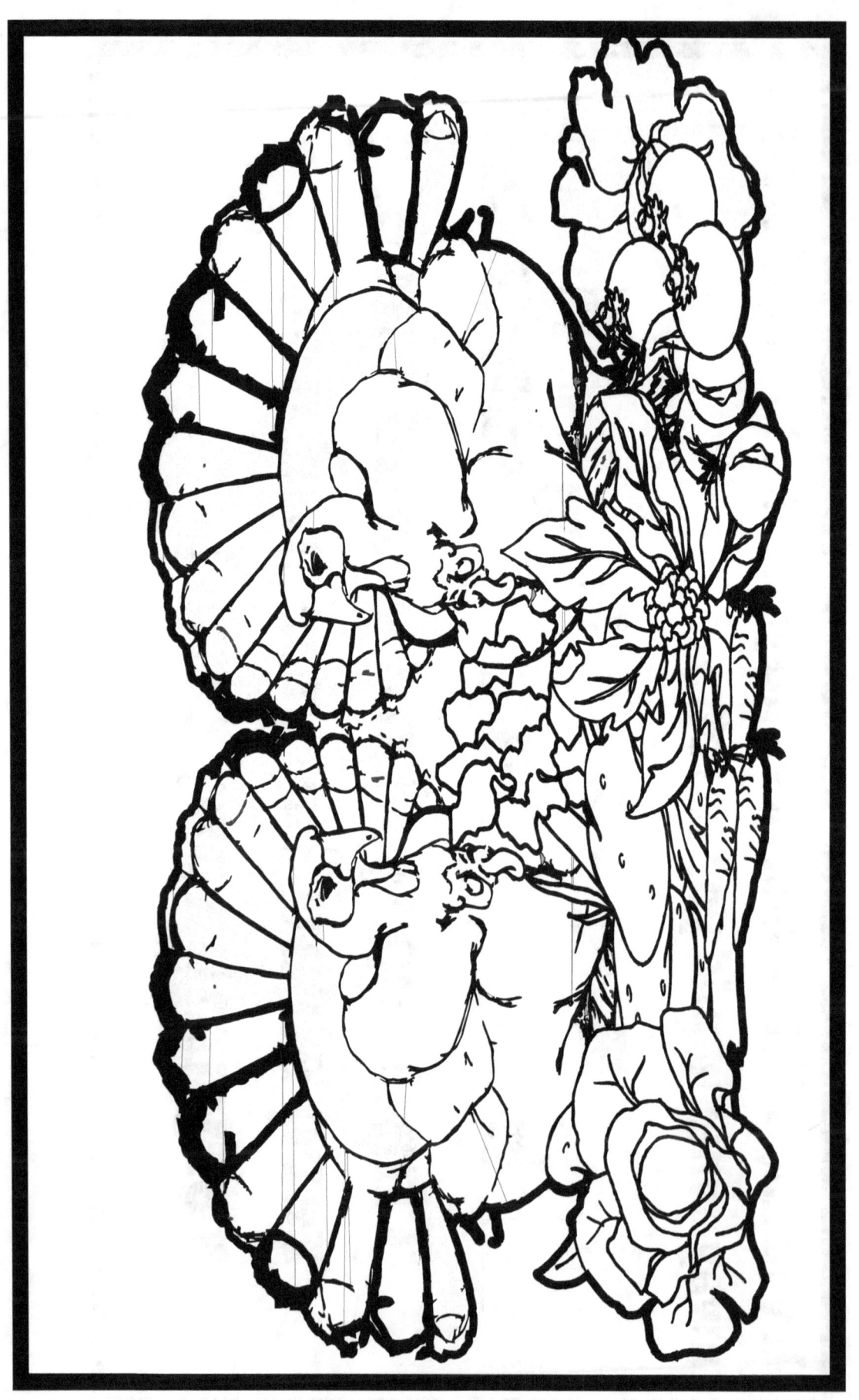

Five and five make _____

ten, but five and _____

a mom and dad _____

make a happy family _____

Unscramble the words to see the message.

www.ingramcontent.com/pod-product-compliance
Lightning Source LLC
Chambersburg PA
CBHW080309180526
45167CB00006B/2730